AF424098
Psychological Warfare: 9/11 as a Tool for Manipulation and Control
by Digby R. Kerr

PSYCHOLOGICAL WARFARE: 9/11 AS A TOOL FOR MANIPULATION AND CONTROL

First edition. September 2, 2024.

Copyright © 2024 Digby R. Kerr.

ISBN: 979-8227973771

Written by Digby R. Kerr.

Also by Digby R. Kerr

The Ripple Effect

The Ripple Effect: "A Fable About Embracing Change and Thriving in Uncertainty"

The Ripple Effect: "A Fable About Embracing Change and Thriving in Uncertainty"

Standalone

The Universal Code: Unlocking the Secrets of Happiness, Wealth, and Health

Mastering LinkedIn: A Comprehensive Guide to Building Your Profile, Growing Your Audience, and Leveraging Business Opportunities

The Universal Code: Unlocking the Secrets of Happiness, Wealth, and Health

Cross-Border Trade Compliance: Navigating the Global Marketplace

Report on Trends and Challenges in Logistics Hiring

"12 Steps to Success: Real-Life Stories of Manifestation and Transformation"

Psychological Warfare: 9/11 as a Tool for Manipulation and Control

Watch for more at https://www.linkedin.com/in/digbyrkerr/.

This book is dedicated to the 2,977 men and women who lost their lives on 9/11. Twenty-three years later, the pain remains as vivid as the memories of that tragic day. We all remember where we were, and the weight of that loss continues to shape our lives. Among the fallen were 343 firefighters, 60 police officers, and 8 paramedics—brave first responders who gave their lives in service to others. Though this book may be controversial, it seeks to honor their memory and the nearly 3,000 souls who perished. Families will never forget, and neither will our nation. May we forever remember their sacrifice.

Chapter 1:
Introduction to Psychological Warfare
Understanding Psychological Warfare

Psychological warfare is a complex and multifaceted concept that encompasses tactics used to influence perception, manipulate beliefs, and control behavior through psychological means rather than direct military action. This subchapter will explore the dynamics of psychological warfare, particularly in the context of the events surrounding September 11, 2001. Understanding psychological warfare is crucial to dissecting how narratives are shaped, especially in the wake of traumatic events. The rami cations of these narratives are profound, as they can drive public opinion, shape policy decisions, and create an enduring atmosphere of fear and mistrust.

In the aftermath of 9/11, a plethora of conspiracy theories emerged, each claiming to uncover hidden truths about the attacks and the alleged involvement of government agencies. These theories often reflect a broader societal skepticism towards governmental institutions, particularly in light of perceived cover-ups and misinformation. For many, the idea that the government could have orchestrated or allowed the attacks to occur taps into deep-seated fears of loss of autonomy and betrayal. This environment of distrust is a fertile ground for psychological warfare, where narratives can be constructed to either reinforce or challenge the official story, manipulating public sentiment and allegiance.

Media manipulation plays a critical role in the context of psychological warfare, especially in how information is disseminated and consumed. The mainstream media's portrayal of the 9/11 attacks shaped public perception in real-time and has continued to influence discourse in the years following. The framing of the narrative —whether it centers on heroism, tragedy, or conspiracy—can evoke specific emotional responses and guide collective memory. The media's choice of language, imagery, and focus can create dichotomies that serve specific agendas, further complicating the public's understanding and response to the events. By analyzing these media narratives, one can discern the psychological tactics employed to maintain control over the public psyche.

Controlled demolition theories, which assert that the Twin Towers and World Trade Center 7 were brought down by explosives rather than the impact of airplanes, illustrate how deeply psychological warfare can intertwine with physical events. These theories appeal to a desire for logical explanations in the face of chaos and tragedy. They challenge the official account and demand a reassessment of the evidence presented to the public. In doing so, they not only provoke critical thinking but also ignite debates over credibility and authority, highlighting the psychological struggle between accepting uncomfortable truths and seeking alternate narratives that provide a sense of order and understanding.

Lastly, the role of the military and the broader implications of psychological operations (psyops) must be considered in understanding the long-term effects of 9/11 on American society. The military's response to the attacks, including preemptive actions and the establishment of a permanent state of alert, can be seen as a continuation of psychological warfare aimed at maintaining control through fear. This response, combined with an analysis of financial motives stemming from the attacks—such as insurance claims and military contracts—creates a narrative where economic interests align with strategic manipulation. Ultimately, the exploration of these themes reveals how psychological warfare operates not only through direct actions but also through the

cultivation of fear, distrust, and a continuous struggle for narrative
dominance in the public sphere.

The Role of Fear in Society

The role of fear in society is a complex and multifaceted phenomenon that has been magnified in the wake of traumatic events such as the September 11 attacks. Fear operates as a powerful psychological tool that can influence public perception, behavior, and ultimately the political landscape. Following 9/11, fear was not merely a reaction; it was strategically utilized by various entities, including governments and media outlets, to shape narratives and elicit compliance from the populace. This manipulation of fear has led to a pervasive atmosphere of distrust, prompting individuals to seek explanations for the attacks that often diverge from official accounts.

In the context of 9/11, fear manifested through a heightened sense of vulnerability and the looming threat of terrorism. This environment cultivated fertile ground for conspiracy theories to flourish, as people sought to make sense of chaotic and devastating events. The narratives surrounding government cover-ups and alleged involvement of agencies in the attacks reflect a deeper societal fear of betrayal by those in power. Such fears are exacerbated by historical precedents where governments have engaged in clandestine activities, further fueling public skepticism and distrust in official explanations.

Mainstream media played a pivotal role in amplifying fear following the attacks, often prioritizing sensationalism over rigorous investigation. The portrayal of terrorism as an omnipresent threat contributed to a climate of anxiety that made individuals more receptive to conspiracy theories. Eyewitness testimonies, which often contradicted the of social narrative, were sometimes dismissed or downplayed, leading to further frustration among those who felt their voices were marginalized. This manipulation of information served to reinforce the power dynamics at play, where fear stirred critical discourse and allowed for the perpetuation of narratives that aligned with governmental interests.

The theories surrounding controlled demolition of the Twin Towers and WTC 7 illustrate how fear can lead to alternative interpretations of evidence. Many individuals, grappling with the shock of the attacks, found solace in the notion that the events could be explained through a lens of deliberate orchestration rather than random acts of violence. This perspective not only reflects a desire for clarity in a chaotic situation but also signifies a profound distrust in the institutions that were expected to protect citizens. The implications of such theories extend beyond mere speculation; they highlight a societal yearning for accountability in a world perceived as increasingly precarious.

Finally, the economic ramifications of 9/11, including military contracts and insurance claims, further underscore the intersection of fear and financial motives. The response of the U.S. military, coupled with allegations of foreknowledge or complicity, has led many to question the true beneficiaries of the attacks. The intertwining of fear with economic interests raises critical questions about the lengths to which entities might go to exploit societal anxieties for profit and control. In this way, the role of fear emerges as not just a reaction to trauma, but as a strategic mechanism for manipulation that continues to reverberate through society, shaping perceptions and influencing behavior long after the dust has settled.

Overview of 9/11 and Its Implications

The events of September 11, 2001, marked a pivotal moment in global history, reshaping the political and social landscape of the United States and beyond. On that fateful day, coordinated terrorist attacks orchestrated by the extremist group al-Qaeda resulted in the destruction of the World Trade Center and signi cant damage to the Pentagon, claiming nearly 3,000 lives. The immediate aftermath saw a surge of fear and uncertainty, leading to heightened security measures and the implementation of policies that prioritized national security over civil liberties. This overview seeks to contextualize the implications of 9/11, particularly in relation to conspiracy theories, government actions, and the role of media in shaping public perception.

In the years following the attacks, various conspiracy theories emerged, suggesting that the official narrative surrounding 9/11 was not only awed but potentially fabricated. These theories range from allegations of government complicity to controlled demolitions of the World Trade Center buildings. The notion that powerful entities may have orchestrated the attacks for ulterior motives resonates with a public increasingly distrustful of government institutions. This skepticism is rooted in historical precedents of government cover-ups and manipulation, which have fueled ongoing debates about the validity of the official accounts of 9/11.

Media coverage of the events of 9/11 played a crucial role in shaping public understanding and response. In the immediate aftermath, mainstream media outlets provided real-time updates that contributed to a narrative of urgency and fear. However, the portrayal of the events also sparked discussions about media manipulation and the framing of the narrative. Critics argue that the media's alignment with government narratives may have limited the scope of dissenting voices, thereby reinforcing the prevailing perspective that framed the attacks as an unprovoked act of terrorism rather than a complex geopolitical event.

The response of the U.S. military to the attacks, including the subsequent wars in Afghanistan and Iraq, raises further questions about the implications of 9/11. Allegations of foreknowledge or complicity among military and intelligence agencies have been a focal point for conspiracy theorists, who argue that the military-industrial complex may have benefited from the chaos. This perspective is fueled by the substantial financial gains realized through military contracts and heightened security measures in the years following the attacks, leading to speculation about whether economic motives played a role in shaping U.S. foreign policy.

The psychological impact of 9/11 cannot be overstated. The pervasive fear and sense of vulnerability that followed the attacks have influenced societal attitudes toward government, security, and international relations. Conspiracy theories often react deep-seated fears and a desire to make sense of a chaotic world, suggesting that individuals seek alternative explanations when faced with overwhelming uncertainty. As these narratives continue to evolve, they serve as a lens through which to examine the broader implications of 9/11, both for individual psychology and for collective societal dynamics.

Chapter 2:
9/11 Conspiracy Theories
Origins of 9/11 Conspiracy Theories

The origins of 9/11 conspiracy theories can be traced back to a complex interplay of societal fears, historical context, and perceived governmental actions. Following the September 11 attacks, a significant segment of the population began to question the official narratives provided by the government and mainstream media. This skepticism was fueled by the immediate aftermath of the tragedy, which saw widespread confusion, misinformation, and a lack of transparency from authorities. As the dust settled, the need for clarity and truth led many individuals to explore alternative explanations, resulting in a proliferation of conspiracy theories that sought to make sense of the chaotic events.

One prominent area of speculation centers around alleged government cover-ups and the involvement of various agencies in the attacks. Many conspiracy theorists argue that elements within the U.S. government, or even the military, had foreknowledge of the attacks or were complicit in their execution. This belief is often supported by claims of inconsistencies and omissions in the official reports, which purportedly raise more questions than they answer. As these theories gained traction, they tapped into a broader narrative of distrust toward government institutions, particularly in the wake of the Iraq War and other controversial decisions made by the U.S. administration.

Media manipulation plays a crucial role in shaping public perception of the 9/11 attacks and the subsequent conspiracy theories. The portrayal of events by mainstream media outlets often reflected governmental narratives, which some critics argue contributed to a lack of critical inquiry into the circumstances surrounding the attacks. The framing of the narrative influenced how the public understood the attacks, leading to the acceptance of certain explanations while marginalizing dissenting voices. This media landscape, characterized by sensationalism and a rush to judgment, laid fertile ground for conspiracy theories to flourish, as individuals sought alternative sources of information that challenged the dominant narrative.

Among the most debated theories is the assertion that the Twin Towers and World Trade Center 7 were brought down by controlled demolitions rather than the impact of the planes. Proponents of this view cite the buildings' rapid collapse and the presence of what they believe to be explosive sounds. These claims often intersect with discussions of eyewitness testimonies, which sometimes contradict the official explanations. The credibility of these accounts is frequently scrutinized, as they can reflect individual perceptions shaped by trauma and the chaos of the moment. Nevertheless, these testimonies have fueled the re of conspiracy theories, illustrating how personal experiences can diverge from established narratives.

The financial motives behind the events of 9/11 further complicate the discourse surrounding conspiracy theories. Economic gains derived from military contracts, as well as insurance claims related to the attacks, have led some theorists to speculate that certain parties may have benefitted from the chaos. This line of thinking dovetails with broader fears about exploitation and manipulation by those in power, emphasizing the psychological impact of fear that emerged in the wake of 9/11. As the landscape of conspiracy theories continues to evolve, it remains essential to critically examine the origins and motivations behind these narratives, recognizing how they reflect the societal anxieties and historical complexities that determine our understanding of this pivotal moment in history.

Key Theories and Their Proponents

The topic of psychological warfare surrounding the events of September 11, 2001, has generated a multitude of theories and interpretations, each with its own set of proponents. This subchapter explores key theories that have emerged in the wake of the attacks, shedding light on the individuals and groups that advocate for them. These theories range from allegations of government complicity to claims of media manipulation, each aiming to decode the complex narrative surrounding 9/11 and its aftermath. Understanding these perspectives is crucial for grasping the broader implications of 9/11 on public perception and societal trust.

One prominent theory centers on alleged government cover-ups, suggesting that various agencies may have had prior knowledge of the attacks or even played a role in orchestrating them. Proponents such as former government officials and independent researchers argue that inconsistencies in official reports and the swift passage of legislation like the Patriot Act indicate a deeper agenda at play. These claims often rely on a combination of circumstantial evidence and selective interpretations of events, contributing to a growing skepticism about the of social narrative provided by the government. The persistence of these theories reflects a significant portion of the population's distrust in governmental institutions, particularly in the context of national security.

Media manipulation is another key theory that has gained traction in discussions about 9/11. Critics argue that mainstream media outlets played a crucial role in shaping public perception through selective reporting and sensationalism. Proponents of this theory, including independent journalists and media analysts, examine how news coverage framed the narrative of the attacks and subsequent wars, often emphasizing fear and urgency. This manipulation purportedly served the interests of those in power, fostering a climate of fear that enabled the government to implement policies without significant public resistance.

By analyzing media narratives, this theory seeks to uncover the mechanisms through which information was controlled and disseminated, influencing societal attitudes toward terrorism and national security.

The controlled demolition theory presents a controversial perspective, claiming that the Twin Towers and World Trade Center 7 were brought down by explosives rather than the impact of the planes. Advocates of this theory include architects, engineers, and conspiracy theorists who argue that the evidence of structural failure contradicts the official explanations. They often cite anomalies such as the speed of the collapses and the presence of molten metal as indicators of a planned demolition. This theory has sparked significant debate within both the engineering community and the general public, raising questions about the integrity of the investigations conducted post-9/11 and the potential for manipulation of scientific evidence to support the official narrative.

Lastly, the theory of psychological operations (psyops) posits that the events of 9/11 were not only a terrorist attack but also a strategic move designed to manipulate public perception and behavior. Proponents of this theory, including social psychologists and military strategists, suggest that the fear generated by the attacks served to rally public support for military interventions and increased surveillance measures. This analysis extends to examining how the psychological impact of 9/11 altered societal norms and fueled conspiracy theories themselves, which often reflect a broader distrust in government and authority. By placing 9/11 within the context of historical psyops, this theory seeks to illustrate how psychological manipulation can shape collective consciousness and influence policy decisions.

In summary, the key theories surrounding 9/11 and their proponents offer a multifaceted view of the events and their aftermath. Each theory reflects specific

societal fears and distrust, as well as the complex interplay between government, media, and public perception. As these theories continue to circulate and evolve, they underscore the enduring impact of 9/11 on American society and the ongoing quest for truth in the face of manipulation and control. Understanding these diverse perspectives is essential for critically engaging with the narratives that shape our collective memory of one of the most consequential events in modern history.

The Ring of Truth: Analyzing Credibility

The concept of credibility in the context of 9/11 conspiracy theories is essential for understanding how narratives are shaped and disseminated. The events of September 11, 2001, serve not only as a significant historical moment but also as a focal point for various interpretations that challenge the official accounts. This subchapter will delve into the intricacies of credibility, analyzing the claims made by conspiracy theorists and the responses from government officials, media outlets, and eyewitnesses. By dissecting the layers of information surrounding 9/11, we can better appreciate how perceptions of truth are constructed and manipulated.

One of the most prominent areas of exploration is the alleged involvement of government agencies in the events of 9/11. Proponents of conspiracy theories argue that certain elements within the U.S. government had foreknowledge of the attacks or may have even facilitated them for political gain. These claims often reference inconsistencies in official narratives and the rapid response of military and intelligence agencies. A critical examination of these assertions reveals the challenges in discerning credible sources and separating fact from speculation. This analysis prompts a broader conversation about the nature of government transparency and accountability, especially in the wake of a national crisis.

Media manipulation plays a crucial role in shaping public perception of 9/11 and its aftermath. The mainstream media's portrayal of the events, the ensuing war on terror, and the narrative surrounding national security has significantly influenced how the public interprets the events of that day. Investigating the framing techniques and the selection of information presented in news coverage sheds light on how narratives can be constructed to support specific agendas. This raises questions about the reliability of mainstream media as a source of truth and the potential consequences of media bias on public understanding.

Claims regarding controlled demolition have gained traction among conspiracy theorists, particularly concerning the collapse of the Twin Towers and World Trade Center 7. Advocates for this theory argue that the buildings exhibited characteristics consistent with a controlled demolition rather than the impact of the airplanes. By examining the scientific and engineering analyses presented by both sides, we can better evaluate the credibility of these claims. The implications of accepting or rejecting such theories extend beyond the technical details, as they tap into deeper societal fears regarding safety, trust in institutions, and the quest for truth in the face of tragedy.

Eyewitness testimonies often serve as a cornerstone for validating or challenging official narratives. However, the credibility of these accounts can be complex and multifaceted. While some eyewitnesses provide compelling details that contradict official reports, others may have their perceptions influenced by trauma, media coverage, or group dynamics. Analyzing the reliability of these testimonies requires a nuanced approach that considers psychological factors, the context of the events, and the potential for selective memory. This exploration highlights the broader theme of how truth is often subjective, shaped by individual experiences and societal narratives, ultimately influencing public discourse and belief systems surrounding the events of 9/11.

Chapter 3:
Government Cover-Ups

Allegations of Government Involvement The subchapter "Allegations of Government Involvement" delves into the intricate web of conspiracy theories surrounding the events of September 11, 2001, focusing on claims that government agencies played a role in orchestrating or facilitating the attacks. Numerous theories have emerged, suggesting that elements within the U.S. government had prior knowledge of the attacks or even actively participated in them. These allegations have captured public attention, fueled by a pervasive distrust in government institutions and the perception that official narratives may be incomplete or misleading.

One of the most prominent aspects of this discussion involves the alleged foreknowledge of the attacks by various government agencies. Critics point to the failure of the FBI, CIA, and other intelligence organizations to prevent the hijackings despite receiving warnings about potential threats. This perceived negligence has led many to speculate whether a more sinister motive was at play. Some theorists argue that a lack of action might have been intentional, suggesting that elements within the government sought to use the attacks as a pretext for military intervention in the Middle East and the implementation of sweeping domestic security measures.

Media manipulation also plays a crucial role in shaping the narrative around government involvement in 9/11. Mainstream media outlets, often criticized for their allegiance to governmental narratives, have been accused of downplaying or dismissing alternative theories. The portrayal of the attacks and their aftermath has been characterized by a focus on patriotism and unity, often overshadowing dissenting voices. This can lead to a cycle of misinformation, where official accounts become accepted without sufficient scrutiny, reinforcing public trust in government while marginalizing alternative perspectives that question the status quo.

Theories surrounding controlled demolition have gained traction among those who argue that the collapse of the Twin Towers and World Trade Center 7 could not have been solely caused by the impact of the planes and subsequent res. Advocates of this theory point to the symmetrical nature of the buildings' collapses and the rapidity with which they fell, suggesting that explosives were planted in advance. Such claims have been met with skepticism from structural engineers and demolition experts, yet they persist in popular discourse, contributing to the broader narrative of government complicity and manipulation.

The economic implications of 9/11 further complicate the discussion of government involvement. Allegations of financial motives have arisen, including claims that certain individuals and organizations stood to profit from the chaos that ensued. Military contracts surged following the attacks, and the insurance claims related to the destruction of the World Trade Center raised questions about who benefited from the tragedy. This intersection of economic interests and governmental actions adds another layer of complexity, suggesting that motivations for involvement may not only be political but also financial in nature. Ultimately, the allegations of government involvement in the events of 9/11 serve as a mirror reflecting societal fears and a profound distrust in authoritative narratives, prompting ongoing debates about accountability, transparency, and the nature of power.

Key Agencies and Their Roles

In the aftermath of the September 11 attacks, various government agencies played crucial roles in both the immediate response and the subsequent investigation. Primarily, the Federal Bureau of Investigation (FBI) and the Central Intelligence Agency (CIA) were at the forefront of national security efforts. The FBI, tasked with domestic intelligence and security, led extensive investigations into the attacks, scrutinizing the actions of the hijackers and any potential connections to broader terrorist networks. Meanwhile, the CIA focused on foreign intelligence gathering, assessing threats from overseas and seeking to identify any international links to the perpetrators. Both agencies, however, faced criticism for alleged lapses in intelligence and communication that may have contributed to the success of the attacks.

Another key player was the Department of Homeland Security (DHS), established shortly after 9/11 to consolidate various aspects of national security and emergency response. The DHS has since been responsible for coordinating efforts to prevent future attacks, which has led to the implementation of controversial policies and practices, such as increased airport security measures and surveillance programs. The creation of this agency not only aimed to enhance national safety but also reflected the heightened atmosphere of fear and suspicion that permeated American society in the wake of the attacks. This atmosphere has fueled a myriad of conspiracy theories, suggesting that the government may have known about the attacks in advance or even facilitated them for political gain.

The military's role in the events surrounding 9/11 cannot be understated. The Department of Defense (DoD) was immediately mobilized to respond to the attacks, launching military operations in Afghanistan against the Taliban and al-Qaeda. However, allegations of foreknowledge or complicity have emerged, with some conspiracy theorists claiming that certain military officials had prior knowledge of the attacks and either allowed them to happen or failed to act decisively to prevent them. This has led to a broader examination of the military-industrial complex and the economic motivations behind the war on terror, as military contracts surged in the aftermath of 9/11, raising questions about the intersection of pro t and national security.

Media coverage of the attacks and their aftermath further complicated public understanding of the events. Mainstream media outlets played a pivotal role in shaping narratives, often reflecting the government's perspective and contributing to a climate of fear and urgency. The framing of the attacks, the portrayal of the perpetrators, and the emphasis on national security concerns all influenced public perception and discourse. Critics argue that this media manipulation has obscured alternative narratives, including those that challenge the official account, such as claims of controlled demolition of the Twin Towers and World Trade Center 7. Eyewitness testimonies have been pivotal in these discussions, with many individuals recounting experiences that contradict the mainstream narrative, thereby complicating the quest for truth.

Finally, the intersection of psychological operations and societal fears following 9/11 has been a fertile ground for conspiracy theories. The trauma and uncertainty felt by the American public created an environment ripe for speculation and distrust, particularly towards government agencies. This distrust has been exacerbated by historical contexts, such as previous government cover-ups and covert operations, which have left many questioning the authenticity of official accounts. Economic motivations, foreign involvement theories, and the role of psychological warfare tactics further illuminate the complexity of the 9/11 narrative. As society grapples with these multifaceted issues, understanding the roles of key agencies provides insight into the broader implications of 9/11 as not just a tragic event, but a pivotal moment in the ongoing struggle for truth, transparency, and accountability in governance.

The Impact of Cover-Ups on Public Trust

The aftermath of 9/11 has profoundly affected public trust in governmental institutions, leading to a pervasive atmosphere of skepticism and suspicion. Coverups, real or perceived, have played a significant role in shaping the narratives surrounding the events of that day. When individuals believe that their government is not being entirely forthcoming, it undermines the foundational trust necessary for a cohesive society. This erosion of trust is particularly pronounced in the context of alleged government involvement in, or complicity with, the events of 9/11, which has fueled a myriad of conspiracy theories that question the very fabric of official accounts.

Media manipulation has also contributed to this phenomenon. In the initial chaos following the attacks, mainstream media outlets were tasked with informing the public, yet their narratives often aligned closely with government pronouncements, raising concerns about journalistic integrity. Critics argue that the media's failure to challenge official narratives created an environment ripe for speculation and conspiracy theories. As the public consumed these narratives, any discrepancies or omissions further fueled suspicions, leading to a widespread belief that there were truths being concealed. This relationship between media reporting and public perception illustrates how narratives can be shaped or distorted, impacting the public's overall trust in the institutions meant to provide accountability.

Theories surrounding controlled demolition of the Twin Towers and WTC 7 represent another critical aspect of this discourse. Proponents of these theories argue that the manner in which the buildings collapsed suggests the use of explosives rather than the impact of the airplanes alone. Such claims, while often dismissed by experts, have gained traction among segments of the population who feel that the official explanations do not adequately address their observations or intuitions. The belief in these alternative explanations not only reflects a distrust in technical and scientific authority, but also signifies a deeper cultural anxiety about government transparency and accountability.

Moreover, the role of the military in the events surrounding 9/11 has been scrutinized, with allegations of foreknowledge and complicity circulating widely. The military's response to the attacks, including the rapid mobilization and subsequent military actions, has led some to question whether there were prior indications of impending threats that were ignored or covered up. This perceived failure to act on available intelligence has perpetuated a narrative of incompetence or worse, conspiracy, further eroding public trust in military institutions. The implications of these theories resonate deeply within a society that values national security, raising uncomfortable questions about the effectiveness and motives of those tasked with protecting it.

Ultimately, the convergence of these elements—government cover-ups, media manipulation, architectural anomalies, military actions, and the resulting societal fears—paints a complex picture of the impact of 9/11 on public trust. Each layer of suspicion compounds the others, creating a feedback loop that reinforces distrust in established narratives. As individuals navigate these contentious waters, the psychological impact of fear becomes evident, with many turning to conspiracy theories as a means of making sense of a chaotic world. Understanding this multifaceted relationship is crucial for addressing the broader implications of 9/11 and its aftermath on public belief systems and institutional trust.

Chapter 4:
Media Manipulation

The Role of Mainstream Media in 9/11 Coverage

The role of mainstream media in the coverage of the September 11 attacks is a critical aspect of understanding the broader implications of the event on public perception and sentiment. In the aftermath of the attacks, media outlets became the primary source of information, shaping narratives that influenced not only the immediate response but also the long-term implications surrounding 9/11. The speed at which news was disseminated, coupled with the emotional weight of the events, created a unique environment that allowed for both factual reporting and the emergence of sensationalized narratives. This duality played a significant role in how the public processed the tragedy and the subsequent government actions.

Mainstream media coverage of 9/11 was characterized by an overwhelming focus on the immediate spectacle of the attacks, with images of the Twin Towers collapsing and chaotic scenes dominating television screens. This relentless focus on the dramatic elements shifted attention away from deeper inquiries into the events themselves and the governmental responses that followed. As the narrative evolved, the media began to present a simplified version of the story, often framing it as a clear-cut battle between good and evil. This binary approach not only influenced public sentiment but also contributed to the creation of a climate of fear, which was later exploited by government agencies to justify various policies, including the War on Terror.

In the months and years that followed 9/11, the mainstream media's portrayal of conspiracy theories further complicated public discourse. While some outlets dismissed alternative narratives outright, others indulged them, often without rigorous examination of the evidence. This inconsistency in coverage allowed for a variety of conspiracy theories to gain traction, including claims of controlled demolitions and foreknowledge by government agencies. By failing to provide thorough investigative journalism on these topics, mainstream media inadvertently legitimized some of the more extreme interpretations of the events, which contributed to a pervasive distrust in official narratives.

Eyewitness testimonies emerged as a crucial component of the media's coverage, providing personal accounts that often contradicted the official story. These testimonies, however, were frequently presented without adequate context or analysis, leading to a fragmented understanding of the events. The media's handling of these accounts often prioritized sensationalism over critical evaluation, thus shaping public perceptions in ways that aligned with existing fears and distrust. As a result, many individuals began to question not only the events of 9/11 but also the integrity of the institutions responsible for reporting on them.

In conclusion, the role of mainstream media in the coverage of 9/11 highlights the complexities of information dissemination in times of crisis. The interplay between sensationalism, emotional appeal, and the quest for narrative clarity created an environment ripe for manipulation and control. As conspiracy theories emerged and flourished in the wake of the attacks, the media's failure to critically engage with these narratives further entangled public perception in a web of fear, suspicion, and uncertainty. Understanding this dynamic is essential for analyzing the psychological warfare that followed 9/11 and its lasting impact on American society and global geopolitics.

Narrative Formation and Control

The concept of narrative formation and control plays a crucial role in understanding the events surrounding 9/11 and the myriad of conspiracy theories that have emerged in its aftermath. In the wake of the attacks, a dominant narrative was swiftly established by government agencies and mainstream media, framing the events as an attack by external terrorists. This narrative not only shaped public perception, but also influenced subsequent discussions surrounding government accountability, media representation, and the motivations behind the attacks. By analyzing how this narrative was constructed and maintained, one can gain insight into the mechanisms of psychological manipulation and control that govern public discourse.

Mainstream media served as a primary vehicle for disseminating the official narrative regarding 9/11. The portrayal of the attacks and the immediate aftermath became a focal point of news coverage, often emphasizing themes of national security and the need for retaliatory measures. This framing effectively marginalized alternative viewpoints, including those of eyewitnesses who reported conflicting accounts. The media's role in reinforcing the government's narrative illustrates how information can be selectively presented to shape public understanding, thereby controlling the narrative landscape. The implications of this manipulation extend beyond 9/11, reflecting broader trends in media representation and the power dynamics in information dissemination.

Conspiracy theories surrounding 9/11, such as claims of controlled demolition or government complicity, highlight the public's growing distrust in official accounts. These theories often arise in environments where individuals feel powerless and seek explanations for complex events. The idea that the Twin Towers and WTC 7 were brought down by explosives rather than the impact of planes not only challenges the official narrative but also reflects a deeper societal fear of losing control over one's safety and security. Investigating these theories requires a careful analysis of the evidence presented, as well as an understanding of the psychological motivations that drive individuals to embrace alternative explanations.

The financial motives related to 9/11 further complicate the narrative, as allegations of insurance claims and military contracts emerge. The aftermath of the attacks saw significant financial shifts, including increased defense spending and the growth of security industries. These economic factors have fueled conspiracy theories suggesting that certain entities may have benefited from the chaos, thereby providing an additional layer of skepticism toward the official narrative. Analyzing these financial implications allows for a more nuanced understanding of how economic interests intersect with national security and public perception.

Ultimately, the exploration of narrative formation and control in the context of 9/11 reveals the intricate interplay between fear, trust, and information. The attacks not only transformed the geopolitical landscape but also reshaped the way individuals process and respond to information. As conspiracy theories continue to flourish, they reflect broader societal anxieties and an enduring quest for truth amid uncertainty. By examining the narratives that have emerged, one can appreciate the importance of critical thinking and the need to question the sources and motivations behind the information that shapes public understanding.

Case Studies of Media Reporting

In examining the media reporting surrounding the events of September 11, 2001, several case studies illustrate the complex interplay between information dissemination and public perception. The immediate aftermath of the attacks saw an unprecedented surge in news coverage, with various outlets competing to present breaking news. This frenzy, often characterized by sensationalism and urgency, laid the groundwork for narratives that would shape public understanding and belief regarding the events. The framing of the attacks, the portrayal of the perpetrators, and the ensuing responses from government and military agencies all played crucial roles in establishing a narrative that would persist for years.

Media coverage of 9/11 was marked by notable inconsistencies, particularly in relation to eyewitness testimonies. Many individuals reported seeing unusual phenomena, such as explosions or secondary blasts, which contradicted the official narrative that attributed the collapses of the Twin Towers and World Trade Center 7 solely to the impact of the aircraft and subsequent res. These testimonies, while often dismissed by mainstream media as unreliable or anecdotal, have fueled conspiracy theories suggesting that controlled demolitions were employed. The dismissal of such accounts raises questions about the media's role in shaping public perception and the extent to which alternative explanations were considered or marginalized.

Furthermore, the media's representation of government agencies during the crisis has been pivotal in discussions about alleged complicity or foreknowledge. Reports highlighting the actions of the military and intelligence communities on the day of the attacks have led to speculation regarding their preparedness and response. For instance, the confusion surrounding the military's protocols for intercepting hijacked planes has prompted inquiries into whether there was a deliberate failure in response or a more sinister involvement. The extent to which the media has investigated these claims, versus promoting a narrative of heroism and quick government action, raises concerns about accountability and transparency.

The financial implications of 9/11 have also been a focus of media analysis, particularly regarding the economic benefits gained by certain sectors. Investigations have revealed a surge in military contracts and insurance claims following the attacks, leading to claims that financial motives may have influenced events or responses. However, mainstream media often downplayed these discussions, focusing instead on immediate human tragedies and national solidarity. This selective reporting may have contributed to a lack of critical examination of the economic landscape following the attacks and how it intertwined with national security policies.

Lastly, the role of psychological operations in the aftermath of 9/11 cannot be overlooked in this context. The media played a significant role in framing the narrative of fear and vulnerability, which in turn influenced public sentiment and policy decisions. By amplifying the notion of an omnipresent threat, the media contributed to a societal environment ripe for manipulation and control. As conspiracy theories emerged, revealing deeper fears and distrust in government, the media's handling of these narratives became a critical factor in how they were received and understood. Collectively, these case studies underscore the need for a more nuanced examination of media reporting on 9/11, acknowledging both its potential to inform and its capacity to mislead.

Chapter 5:
Controlled Demolition Theories

Overview of Controlled Demolition Claims

The subchapter "Overview of Controlled Demolition Claims" delves into a prominent aspect of the 9/11 conspiracy theories, focusing on assertions that the destruction of the Twin Towers and World Trade Center 7 (WTC 7) was not solely the result of the impact from hijacked airplanes but was instead the product of preplanned controlled demolitions. This theory gained traction in the aftermath of the attacks, fueled by a combination of eyewitness accounts, perceived anomalies in the buildings' collapses, and the public's growing skepticism towards official narratives. Such claims serve as a lens through which broader societal fears and distrust in government actions can be understood.

Proponents of controlled demolition theories often cite the manner in which the buildings fell—particularly the rapid, symmetrical collapse of WTC 7, which was not directly hit by a plane. Critics of the official explanation argue that the characteristics of these collapses resemble those of traditional demolitions, where explosives are strategically placed to ensure a swift and complete failure of a structure. The discussion surrounding these claims not only highlights the complexities of structural engineering but also underscores the importance of transparency in the investigation processes following such monumental events. The interplay of expert opinions and layperson observations creates a rich tapestry of debate that continues to evolve.

Eyewitness testimonies play a crucial role in the controlled demolition narrative. Some witnesses reported hearing explosions during the events of 9/11, describing sounds reminiscent of dynamite. Such accounts, while compelling, raise questions regarding their reliability, context, and the psychological state of individuals witnessing chaotic and traumatic events. The impact of fear and confusion on perception cannot be understated, as the stress of the situation may lead individuals to interpret sensory information in ways that align with their pre-existing beliefs or fears. This phenomenon highlights the need for a critical examination of how eyewitness accounts can both challenge and reinforce narratives.

The media's portrayal of the 9/11 attacks has also significantly influenced public perception of controlled demolition theories. Mainstream news outlets initially reported on the events as they unfolded, but the subsequent coverage often reinforced official narratives without adequately addressing alternative explanations. This lack of comprehensive discourse has contributed to the emergence of conspiracy theories as individuals seek out alternative sources of information that challenge the status quo. The role of media manipulation in shaping public understanding is pivotal, as it can either validate or undermine the claims made by various groups, including those advocating for controlled demolition theories.

Finally, the financial implications of 9/11 cannot be overlooked when examining controlled demolition claims. The attacks triggered a cascade of economic consequences, including increased military spending, security contracts, and insurance payouts related to the destruction of the World Trade Center. Some conspiracy theorists argue that these financial motives could provide a rationale for a staged event, suggesting that those in power may have bene ted from the chaos. The exploration of financial motives in conjunction with controlled demolition theories reflects a broader societal concern regarding the potential for exploitation of fear and tragedy for personal or political gain, further fueling the cycle of distrust and speculation surrounding the events of 9/11.

Scientific Analysis of Collapse Mechanics

The scientific analysis of collapse mechanics, particularly regarding the events of September 11, 2001, has been a focal point of both forensic investigation and public discourse. Understanding the physical forces at play during the collapse of the Twin Towers and World Trade Center 7 is crucial for evaluating the validity of various theories surrounding these events. Engineers and architects have conducted extensive studies to analyze the structural integrity of the buildings, the impact of the aircraft, and the subsequent res that contributed to the catastrophic failures. This analysis provides a foundation for understanding not only the mechanics of the collapses but also the implications for public perception and conspiracy theories.

The official investigations, including the National Institute of Standards and Technology (NIST) report, concluded that the impacts of the planes, combined with the resulting fire, caused the structural failures. The report detailed how the intense heat weakened the steel beams, leading to a progressive collapse. However, this explanation has been met with skepticism from various groups who argue that the physics of the collapses do not align with the observed behaviors of the buildings. Proponents of controlled demolition theories suggest that the symmetrical nature of the collapses and the speed at which they occurred are more consistent with explosive interventions than with re-induced failures. These contrasting analyses fuel ongoing debates about the credibility of of cial narratives.

Eyewitness testimonies play a critical role in shaping public perceptions of the collapse mechanics. Many individuals reported hearing explosions and witnessing unusual events leading up to and during the collapses. These accounts often contradict the conclusions drawn by official investigations and have become integral to conspiracy theories suggesting that a controlled demolition was at play. Evaluating the credibility of these testimonies is complex, as factors such as trauma, confusion, and the chaotic nature of the event can influence individual perceptions. This highlights the psychological aspect of how narratives are formed and spread, further complicating the scientific understanding of the events.

Additionally, the historical context surrounding 9/11 reveals underlying factors that may have influenced both the events of that day and the subsequent narratives. The relationship between the U.S. government and various foreign entities, along with previous military engagements, creates a backdrop of suspicion and distrust. Claims of foreknowledge or complicity among government agencies are often rooted in this historical context, as well as in the financial motives that followed the attacks. The economic rami cations, such as insurance payouts and increased military contracts, add another dimension to the analysis of collapse mechanics, suggesting that financial interests may have influenced public and governmental responses to the crisis.

Ultimately, the analysis of collapse mechanics serves as a lens through which broader themes of manipulation and control can be examined. The technical assessments of structural failures, combined with the exploration of conspiracy theories and psychological operations, reveal how fear and distrust can shape societal beliefs. In a world where information is often contested, understanding the scientific principles behind the collapses and the narratives that emerge is essential for fostering informed discussions about 9/11 and its lasting impact on public consciousness.

Comparisons with Official Explanations

In the wake of the 9/11 attacks, a multitude of narratives emerged, each attempting to explain the events of that fateful day. While the official explanations provided by the U.S. government have been widely accepted, they have also been met with skepticism and alternative theories. This subchapter aims to compare these official accounts with various conspiracy theories that have gained traction over time. The divergences between the two highlight not only the complexities of the event but also the broader societal implications of belief in conspiracy theories, revealing deeper anxieties and distrust in government institutions.

Official explanations assert that 19 hijackers, motivated by extremist ideology, executed a coordinated attack using commercial airliners as weapons. This narrative has been supported by extensive investigations, including the 9/11 Commission Report. However, many skeptics argue that the official narrative oversimplifies the intricate web of events leading up to and following the attacks. For some, this perceived lack of depth in the government's account has fueled alternative theories, suggesting that elements within the government may have had foreknowledge of the attacks or even facilitated them for political gain. This notion of complicity raises questions about the veracity of official statements and the motivations behind them.

Media coverage of the events also played a crucial role in shaping public perception. The mainstream media's portrayal of the attacks and their aftermath often aligned closely with the official narrative. However, critics argue that this alignment may have led to a lack of critical inquiry into alternative explanations. The rapid dissemination of information, coupled with sensational reporting, may have inadvertently stymied discussion on the possibility of controlled demolitions or other forms of manipulation. Eyewitness testimonies that contradicted the official accounts were often marginalized, suggesting a possible bias in media reporting that favored the government's explanations while sidelining dissenting voices.

The theories surrounding controlled demolitions of the Twin Towers and World Trade Center 7 also deserve attention in this context. Proponents of these theories argue that the manner of the buildings' collapse was consistent with a controlled demolition rather than the impact of the planes alone. This perspective challenges the established narrative and raises critical questions regarding architectural integrity, emergency response, and the investigative processes following the attacks. Such claims highlight the complexities involved in the analysis of the events and the need for a thorough examination of all evidence, including that which contradicts the official story.

Finally, the financial motives that emerged post-9/11 provide another layer of complexity to the discussion. Some conspiracy theorists suggest that various stakeholders, including government agencies and private contractors, stood to bene t economically from the chaos. The surge in military contracts and the insurance claims following the attacks have been cited as evidence of potential ulterior motives. This nancial lens offers insights into how economic interests align with narratives of manipulation and control, further feeding the public's fear and distrust. Ultimately, the comparisons between official explanations and alternative theories surrounding 9/11 reflect a broader societal struggle to understand the events and their implications, highlighting the importance of critical thinking and informed discourse in navigating these complex issues.

Chapter 6: The Role of the Military U.S. Military Response on September 11

The U.S. military's response to the September 11 attacks represents a pivotal moment in American history, marked by immediate actions that were both reactive and strategic. On that fateful day, as the nation was engulfed in chaos following the hijacking of four commercial airliners, the military was thrust into a state of high alert. NORAD (North American Aerospace Defense Command) scrambled fighter jets in an unprecedented response to intercept the hijacked planes, although these efforts were hampered by the sheer speed and unpredictability of the attacks. This rapid mobilization raises questions about the military's preparedness and the extent to which it had anticipated such a scenario, a topic that has fueled various conspiracy theories suggesting foreknowledge or complicity.

In the aftermath, the U.S. military's role evolved dramatically as the nation shifted from defense to offense. Within weeks, the U.S. launched Operation Enduring Freedom, a military campaign aimed at dismantling the Taliban regime in Afghanistan and targeting al-Qaeda operatives. This military response was framed not only as a protective measure for national security but also as a means of demonstrating strength and resolve to both domestic and international audiences. The rapid deployment of troops and equipment highlighted the military's capacity for mobilization but also raised concerns about the potential for overreach and the motivations driving U.S. foreign policy in the post-9/11 era.

The media played a crucial role in shaping public perception of the military's response. Mainstream narratives often portrayed the military as a heroic force standing against terrorism, reinforcing a binary view of good versus evil. However, critical analyses reveal that media reporting frequently overlooked or simplified the complexities surrounding the military's engagements and the geopolitical implications of its actions. This manipulation of information has contributed to the growth of conspiracy theories, as many individuals began to question the accuracy and integrity of official narratives, fostering a climate of distrust in both the government and the media.

Additionally, the military's aggressive response to 9/11 has been scrutinized in the context of financial motives. The subsequent wars in Afghanistan and Iraq resulted in significant military contracts and lucrative opportunities for defense contractors. Critics argue that these economic interests may have influenced the decision-making processes within the government and military establishment, further fueling conspiracy theories regarding the true motivations behind the military's actions. The intertwining of military operations and economic gain raises important ethical questions about accountability and transparency in the face of national crises.

The psychological ramifications of the military response also warrant examination. The immediate and overwhelming show of force was intended to instill confidence in the American populace, yet it also played into broader societal fears regarding terrorism and vulnerability. The use of military might as a tool for psychological operations (psyops) can be seen as both a means of control and a method for rallying public support for ongoing military engagements. This interplay between fear, manipulation, and the military's response reflects a complex landscape in which the events of 9/11 have continued to shape American policy and public perception, leaving a lasting legacy that continues to inspire debate and inquiry.

Foreknowledge and Complicity Claims

The subchapter "Foreknowledge and Complicity Claims" explores the intricate web of theories surrounding the events of September 11, 2001, particularly focusing on the alleged foreknowledge and complicity of various entities, including government agencies. These claims suggest that certain of officials or organizations may have had prior knowledge of the attacks and failed to act or even facilitated the events for ulterior motives. Such assertions tap into deep-seated societal fears and distrust of governmental authority, particularly in the wake of significant tragedies where the populace seeks answers beyond official narratives.

One of the core elements of the foreknowledge claims involves the behavior of government agencies prior to the attacks. Critics point to various warnings and intelligence reports that indicated a heightened risk of terrorist activity against the United States. The failure to prevent the attacks, despite these warnings, has led to speculation about whether there was a deliberate decision to allow the attacks to occur or whether agencies were simply negligent. This narrative posits that such foreknowledge could have been used to justify subsequent military actions and domestic policy shifts, ultimately serving the interests of those in power.

Furthermore, the media's role in shaping public perception of these claims cannot be understated. Mainstream news outlets were often criticized for their rapid acceptance of official narratives without adequate scrutiny. The framing of the attacks and the ensuing War on Terror created a backdrop that marginalized dissenting voices and alternative theories. The way information was disseminated, and the language used to describe the events contributed to a societal climate where questioning the government's narrative became synonymous with being labeled a conspiracy theorist. This dynamic further complicated the discourse surrounding foreknowledge and complicity claims, as many felt compelled to reconcile their disbelief with the information presented by trusted media sources.

Theories surrounding controlled demolition of the Twin Towers and World Trade Center 7 add another layer to the foreknowledge discussion. Proponents of this theory argue that the manner of the buildings' collapse suggests pre-planned demolitions rather than the result of impact from the hijacked planes. This claim is often bolstered by eyewitness testimonies and expert analyses that challenge the official accounts. Such theories not only raise questions about the physical evidence but also imply a deeper level of complicity—suggesting that individuals within the government or military may have been involved in orchestrating or covering up the true nature of the attacks.

Lastly, the financial implications of 9/11 and the subsequent War on Terror serve as a crucial element in understanding the motivations behind potential foreknowledge and complicity. The economic windfall for defense contractors and the insurance payouts following the attacks have led some to theorize that there were financial incentives for certain parties to allow the attacks to occur. This perspective posits that the horrors of 9/11 were not merely terrorist acts but calculated moves within a larger strategy of manipulation and control, where fear was weaponized to justify military actions and enhance economic gains. The interplay of these factors underscores a complex narrative that continues to resonate within discussions of 9/11-related conspiracy theories, reflecting broader societal anxieties about authority and accountability in times of crisis.

The Military-Industrial Complex and 9/11

The concept of the military-industrial complex, which describes the relationship between a country's military and the defense industry that supplies it, plays a crucial role in understanding the events surrounding September 11, 2001. Following the attacks, the United States experienced a significant shift in its military and foreign policy, characterized by increased defense spending and a global military presence. This relationship has led some to speculate about the motivations behind the attacks, suggesting that they served as a catalyst for the expansion of military operations and the bolstering of defense contracts. The invocation of national security in the aftermath of 9/11 created an environment where the military-industrial complex thrived, raising questions about whether the attacks were exploited to further specific economic and geopolitical agendas.

Allegations of government complicity or foreknowledge have become central to many conspiracy theories surrounding 9/11. Critics argue that certain government agencies, including the CIA and FBI, may have had advance knowledge of the attacks but failed to act on that information, whether due to incompetence or a more sinister motive. The chaotic response to the attacks and the subsequent wars in Afghanistan and Iraq have fueled suspicions that the government manipulated the situation to justify military engagement and to satisfy the interests of defense contractors. The intertwining of military objectives with national narratives about terrorism has led to a pervasive belief among some segments of the population that the government may have orchestrated or allowed the events of 9/11 to unfold for ulterior motives.

Media coverage of the 9/11 attacks also plays a significant role in shaping public perception and fueling conspiracy theories. In the immediate aftermath, mainstream media outlets provided extensive coverage of the events, often framed within a narrative of heroism and national unity. However, as the years progressed, alternative narratives began to emerge, highlighting discrepancies in official accounts and eyewitness testimonies. The media's role in amplifying certain perspectives while marginalizing others has contributed to a climate of distrust. By failing to critically analyze the government's response and the military's involvement, mainstream media may have inadvertently reinforced the notion that a cover-up exists, thus legitimizing conspiracy theories in the eyes of skeptics.

Theories surrounding controlled demolition have gained traction in the years following 9/11, particularly regarding the Twin Towers and World Trade Center 7. Proponents of these theories argue that the manner in which the buildings collapsed resembled controlled demolitions rather than the result of impact from the hijacked planes. Investigations, including those conducted by the National Institute of Standards and Technology (NIST), have contested these claims, attributing the collapses to re-induced structural damage. Nonetheless, the persistence of controlled demolition theories underscores a broader societal fear and skepticism regarding the official narrative, illustrating how deeply ingrained distrust in government and institutions can shape public discourse.

The financial implications of 9/11 also warrant examination, as the events generated significant economic repercussions that benefited the military-industrial complex. In the wake of the attacks, defense spending surged, and new military contracts were awarded, leading to substantial profits for corporations in the defense sector. Additionally, insurance claims related to the destruction of the World Trade Center created a financial windfall for certain industries. This nexus of military, corporate, and governmental interests raises critical questions about the motives behind the U.S. response to 9/11 and whether the tragedy was manipulated to facilitate economic gain. The intertwining of fear, manipulation, and financial incentives illustrates how 9/11 has served as a focal point for examining the dynamics of power and control within society.

Chapter 7:
Financial Motives
Economic Impact of 9/11

The economic impact of the September 11 attacks in 2001 was both immediate and profound, reverberating across various sectors and reshaping the landscape of American society. The destruction of the World Trade Center not only resulted in the tragic loss of thousands of lives but also initiated significant damage to the economy. In the immediate aftermath, businesses in Lower Manhattan faced crippling losses, with estimates suggesting that insurance claims related to the attacks exceeded $40 billion. The impact extended beyond physical destruction; the psychological impact of fear and uncertainty led to a decline in consumer confidence, resulting in reduced spending and investment. This economic downturn contributed to a recession that lasted for several months, highlighting how a singular catastrophic event can have far-reaching economic consequences.

In the years following 9/11, the U.S. government initiated extensive military operations in Afghanistan and later Iraq, which further fueled economic shifts. Defense spending surged to unprecedented levels, leading to lucrative contracts for defense contractors and related industries. This influx of government spending was often justified under the guise of national security, but it also raised questions about the financial motives behind such military actions. Critics argue that a significant portion of the economic gains from the post-9/11 military endeavors disproportionately benefited a select group of corporations, creating a perception that the attacks and subsequent wars were exploited for financial gain. This narrative has been further complicated by allegations of government complicity, suggesting that certain agencies may have had foreknowledge of the attacks and their economic rami cations.

The media's role in shaping the narrative surrounding 9/11 also had economic implications. Mainstream media coverage focused heavily on the immediate aftermath of the attacks and the ensuing military actions, often portraying them as necessary responses to a clear and present danger. This framing helped to legitimize increased government spending in defense and security, as well as the expansion of surveillance measures. However, the media's portrayal of the events also fostered an environment of fear, which had a chilling effect on the economy by deterring tourism and investment in major urban areas. The lingering effects of this fear, coupled with a distrust in government motives, have fueled conspiracy theories that suggest the economic benefits derived from the attacks played a role in shaping the official narrative.

Theories surrounding controlled demolition have also emerged, positing that the collapses of the Twin Towers and World Trade Center 7 were not solely the result of plane impacts and res but rather orchestrated demolitions. Proponents of these theories argue that such an operation would require significant financial investment and planning, indicating a potential financial motive behind the events of 9/11. This perspective raises questions about the economic interests that may have been served by the destruction of these buildings, including the potential for lucrative reconstruction contracts and real estate developments in the aftermath of the attacks. Such theories challenge the accepted narratives and highlight the intricate connections between economic interests and the events of that fateful day.

Ultimately, the economic impact of 9/11 is intertwined with broader themes of manipulation and control. The interplay between government actions, media narratives, and economic consequences reflects the complexities of societal fear and the erosion of trust. As conspiracy theories continue to circulate, they serve as a lens through which individuals analyze not only the events of 9/11 but also the motivations behind them. The legacy of the attacks extends beyond the immediate loss of life and property; it encompasses a reddened economic landscape shaped by fear, distrust, and the relentless pursuit of power and profit in the wake of tragedy.

Insurance Claims and Payouts

Insurance claims and payouts following the September 11 attacks serve as a compelling case study in the intersection of financial motives and crisis response. The aftermath of the attacks generated a substantial wave of insurance claims from various sectors, including property, business interruption, and life insurance. The destruction of the World Trade Center complex, along with the damage inflicted on surrounding properties, led to payouts that reached into the billions. This financial dimension raises critical questions about the motivations behind such large-scale insurance claims and the implications for both the insurance industry and public perception of the events.

The role of the insurance industry in the wake of 9/11 is often scrutinized within the context of alleged government cover-ups and conspiracy theories. Investigations into the claims led reveal a complicated web of policy details and negotiations that suggest a pre-existing knowledge of potential attacks among certain entities. The timing of these claims, combined with the significant financial interests at stake, has led some conspiracy theorists to speculate about the possibility of collusion between government agencies and insurance companies. These allegations point to a broader narrative that suggests a manipulation of events for financial gain, thereby deepening public distrust in official accounts.

Media manipulation played a pivotal role in shaping the narrative surrounding the insurance claims resulting from 9/11. Mainstream media outlets focused heavily on human interest stories and the immediate aftermath of the attacks, often sidelining the complex financial rami cations. This selective reporting may have contributed to a lack of critical examination of the insurance industry's role in the aftermath. By framing the narrative primarily around heroism and tragedy, the media may have inadvertently obscured potential financial motivations and the intricacies of the claims process, leaving room for speculation and conspiracy theories to flourish.

The financial motives behind the insurance claims also intersect with broader themes of fear and control within society. The traumatic impact of 9/11 instilled a pervasive sense of vulnerability, leading to an environment where fear can be exploited. This fear was not only a catalyst for immediate economic responses but also served as a tool for manipulation by various actors, including the government and private enterprises. In the wake of such a catastrophic event, public sentiment often sways towards accepting narratives that promote security measures and military actions, which in turn benefits those with vested interests, including defense contractors and insurers.

Lastly, examining the insurance claims within the context of psychological operations (psyops) reveals a multifaceted approach to understanding 9/11 and its aftermath. The concept of psyops involves the strategic use of information to influence public perception and behavior, and the handling of insurance claims can be viewed through this lens. By controlling the narrative around financial compensation and the recovery process, various stakeholders could reinforce certain societal fears while simultaneously promoting a narrative that aligns with their interests. This dynamic interplay highlights how financial crises can be woven into larger psychological operations, ultimately shaping public perception and trust in institutions long after the immediate events have passed.

Military Contracts and Economic Gains

The subchapter "Military Contracts and Economic Gains" delves into the intricate relationship between the events of September 11, 2001, and the subsequent surge in military contracts and economic opportunities that arose in the wake of the attacks. This relationship is not merely a byproduct of the tragedy but reflects a broader pattern of how crises can serve as catalysts for economic gain, particularly within the defense sector. Following 9/11, the U.S. government allocated substantial resources to national security, resulting in an unprecedented boom for defense contractors. This financial influx has raised questions about the motivations behind military engagements and the extent to which economic interests can influence governmental policy.

In the aftermath of 9/11, the U.S. government initiated a comprehensive response that included the wars in Afghanistan and Iraq. These military operations necessitated rapid procurement of weapons, technology, and services, which in turn fueled a significant increase in military contracts. The Department of Defense's budget swelled, and companies that provided everything from cybersecurity to logistics services benefited immensely. This dynamic has led critics to argue that the military-industrial complex not only capitalizes on national tragedies but also plays a role in shaping the narrative surrounding military interventions. The economic motivations behind these contracts can raise ethical concerns, prompting discussions about the prioritization of profit over human lives.

Additionally, the economic impact of 9/11 extended beyond military contracts. The attacks prompted a wave of insurance claims that affected various sectors, including airlines and tourism. However, the most poignant economic gains can be traced back to the defense industry. Following the attacks, companies like Halliburton and Lockheed Martin saw their revenues soar as the government sought to enhance national security measures. This aspect of the post-9/11 economy is often overlooked in discussions about the implications of the attacks, yet it is crucial to understanding how financial incentives can shape policy decisions and public perception.

The intertwining of military contracts and economic interests also invites scrutiny regarding the role of government agencies. Allegations of foreknowledge or complicity in the attacks often suggest that certain entities may have benefited from the chaos that ensued. Critics argue that the government's response to 9/11, including the passage of the Patriot Act and the expansion of surveillance programs, was influenced by the financial interests of powerful defense contractors. This raises questions about transparency and accountability in the decision-making processes that govern national security, as well as the potential for conflicts of interest to arise in such a politically charged environment.

Ultimately, the connections between military contracts and economic gains post9/11 reflect broader societal fears and distrust in government institutions. As conspiracy theories proliferate, they often highlight misunderstandings about the motivations behind military actions and the relationship between government and private enterprise. Understanding these economic dimensions is essential to grasping the full impact of 9/11 on American society, as it reveals how fear and crisis can be manipulated to serve both political and financial ends. In unraveling the complexities of military contracts and their implications, we gain insight into the psychological operations at play and the lasting effects of September 11 on the American psyche.

Chapter 8:
The Impact of Fear
Societal Fears Post-9/11

The events of September 11, 2001, catalyzed a profound transformation in American society, instigating a wave of fears that permeated various aspects of life. In the aftermath of the attacks, a climate of uncertainty emerged, characterized by heightened anxiety concerning national security, terrorism, and the reliability of governmental institutions. This societal fear was not merely a response to the immediate violence of the day; it reflected deeper anxieties about vulnerability, trust, and the potential for manipulation by those in power. As a result, public discourse increasingly gravitated toward conspiracy theories, suggesting a pervasive distrust in official narratives and a search for alternative explanations.

One significant aspect of societal fears post-9/11 is the suspicion surrounding government involvement or complicity in the attacks. Several conspiracy theories have emerged, speculating on the role of government agencies in either facilitating the events or failing to prevent them. These theories tap into a historical context of distrust, particularly in the wake of controversial government actions, such as the Gulf of Tonkin incident or the Watergate scandal. The belief that the government could be involved in orchestrating such a catastrophic event feeds into broader fears about the integrity of national leadership and the potential for manipulation at the highest levels.

Media manipulation played a crucial role in shaping public perceptions of 9/11 and its aftermath. The mainstream media's coverage often emphasized sensational aspects of the attacks while downplaying or ignoring dissenting voices and alternative narratives. This selective reporting contributed to a monolithic understanding of the events and fostered an environment in which conspiracy theories could flourish. By presenting a singular narrative, the media not only influenced the public's immediate reaction to the attacks but also shaped long-term perceptions of the government's motives and actions. The resulting distrust in media sources further exacerbated societal fears, leading individuals to seek out alternative information channels.

Conspiracy theories surrounding controlled demolitions of the Twin Towers and World Trade Center 7 serve as a stark illustration of how fear manifests in the search for explanations that align with personal beliefs. Eyewitness testimonies claiming to have heard explosions before the buildings collapsed contradict official accounts, fueling skepticism about the narrative presented by authorities. This skepticism is compounded by the perception that critical information is often suppressed, leading individuals to question the credibility of both eyewitness accounts and of cial reports. The intertwining of fear, distrust, and the desire for clarity illustrates how post-9/11 society has navigated the complex emotional landscape shaped by trauma and uncertainty.

Lastly, the economic rami cations of 9/11 have not gone unnoticed, with discussions surrounding financial motives becoming increasingly prevalent. The surge in military contracts and insurance claims post-attacks raises questions about the potential exploitation of the tragedy for pro t. This financial dimension intertwines with societal fears, suggesting that the motivations for the attacks or the responses to them may have been influenced by economic factors. By examining these connections, it becomes evident that the societal fears post-9/11 extend beyond immediate security concerns to encompass broader anxieties about control, manipulation, and the integrity of societal institutions. In this context, 9/11 serves not only as a historical event but also as a psychological operation that continues to resonate through societal fears and distrust.

Distrust in Government and Institutions

Distrust in government and institutions has been a defining feature of the post-9/11 landscape, shaping public perceptions and fueling various conspiracy theories. The tragic events of September 11, 2001, not only resulted in loss of life but also left a profound impact on the collective psyche of the American populace. The ensuing narratives surrounding the attacks have often been punctuated by skepticism, leading many to question the motives and actions of government agencies. This skepticism has, in turn, fostered an environment ripe for conspiracy theories, some of which suggest that elements within the government may have either orchestrated or facilitated the attacks for ulterior motives.

Central to the discourse on distrust is the perception of government cover-ups. Allegations have emerged suggesting that certain government agencies possessed prior knowledge of the attacks yet failed to act, or worse, actively participated in the orchestration of events. This belief is often fueled by the revelations of intelligence failures, such as the inability of agencies to effectively share information that could have potentially thwarted the attacks. These gaps in accountability create fertile ground for conspiracy theories, as they imply an intentional withholding of truth, leading citizens to question the integrity and transparency of the very institutions meant to protect them.

Media manipulation also plays a significant role in shaping public distrust. In the wake of 9/11, mainstream media outlets were criticized for their reporting, which many argued was overly reliant on government sources and narratives. This alignment raised concerns about the objectivity of the news and the potential for propaganda. Furthermore, the portrayal of the attacks and subsequent security measures often lacked critical scrutiny, leading to a perception that the media served as a mouthpiece for government narratives rather than an independent watchdog. As a result, many citizens began to view mainstream media as complicit in the dissemination of potentially misleading information, further eroding trust in both the media and government.

The claims surrounding controlled demolition theories, particularly regarding the collapse of the Twin Towers and World Trade Center 7, highlight how deeply distrust can influence public perception. Proponents of these theories argue that the manner in which the buildings fell resembled controlled demolitions, suggesting pre-planned actions rather than the result of the impact from the hijacked planes. This assertion taps into the broader societal fear of hidden agendas and manipulations, reinforcing the idea that entities within the government may have orchestrated a scenario that served their interests. Such theories gain traction particularly in environments where information is scarce or contradictory, making it easier for alternative explanations to take root.

The impact of fear is another crucial element in understanding the distrust that characterizes the aftermath of 9/11. The attacks instilled a profound sense of vulnerability, leading to an increased appetite for explanations that provide a semblance of control over an uncontrollable situation. Conspiracy theories, while often lacking rigorous evidence, offer narratives that resonate with societal fears, suggesting that larger forces are at play in orchestrating events. This tendency to search for hidden truths reflects a broader psychological response to trauma, wherein individuals may find solace in believing that they are not merely passive victims but rather active participants in uncovering darker realities. In this context, distrust becomes not just a reaction to specific events but a lens through which many view the world, shaping their understanding of government, media, and the narratives that surround them.

Conspiracy Theories as a Coping Mechanism

Conspiracy theories surrounding significant events often serve as a psychological coping mechanism for individuals grappling with the complexities and traumas of those events. The attacks on September 11, 2001, which resulted in profound loss and national upheaval, are no exception. In the aftermath of this tragedy, many turned to conspiracy theories as a way to make sense of an incomprehensible reality. By proposing alternative narratives, these theories provide a semblance of control and understanding in a world that suddenly felt chaotic and threatening.

The allure of conspiracy theories can be attributed to several psychological factors, including a fundamental need for explanation and certainty in the face of fear. After 9/11, the public was inundated with information, much of it conflicting or incomplete. This lack of clarity can amplify feelings of vulnerability, leading individuals to seek out simpler, more digestible explanations. Conspiracy theories often offer a clear culprit or a nefarious agenda, which can feel more comforting than the chaotic randomness of a terrorist attack. In this way, they can fulfill a psychological need for closure and understanding.

Moreover, conspiracy theories can reflect a deep-seated distrust in institutions, particularly government and media. The events of 9/11 exposed vulnerabilities in national security and prompted widespread criticism of governmental preparedness. Many theories suggest that government agencies either had foreknowledge of the attacks or were complicit in them, feeding into a narrative of betrayal and manipulation. This skepticism is further fueled by instances of real government cover-ups throughout history, leading individuals to draw parallels and question the official accounts. The media's role in shaping the narrative around 9/11 also contributed to this distrust. As mainstream outlets presented their interpretations of the events, inconsistencies and sensationalism saw many citizens turning to alternative narratives that they perceived as more credible.

The specific claims made by conspiracy theorists often reflect broader societal fears and anxieties. For instance, theories surrounding controlled demolitions of the Twin Towers and World Trade Center 7 highlight a fear of loss of control and the potential for manipulation by powerful entities. The idea that these iconic structures could be deliberately destroyed, rather than falling victim to an external attack, suggests a betrayal of the public's trust in safety and security. This narrative serves to reinforce a perception of vulnerability in a society that values resilience and protection, further fueling the need for alternative explanations.

Eyewitness testimonies play a crucial role in the proliferation of conspiracy theories, as they often contradict official narratives and provide anecdotal evidence that challenges the accepted story. The credibility of these accounts varies, yet they resonate deeply with those looking for validation of their suspicions. In the context of 9/11, such testimonies can bolster conspiracy theories related to foreign involvement or military complicity, feeding into the overarching sentiment of betrayal. By framing the narrative in terms of personal experience and perceived injustice, these theories become more compelling and accessible to those seeking to understand the tragedy.

In conclusion, conspiracy theories surrounding 9/11 illustrate how individuals cope with trauma and uncertainty in their lives. They serve as a psychological refuge, offering alternative narratives that provide clarity and meaning amid chaos. These theories not only re ect individual anxieties and distrust but also highlight broader societal fears about vulnerability and manipulation. Understanding the psychological underpinnings of these beliefs is essential for comprehending their persistence and influence in the public discourse surrounding 9/11 and its aftermath.

Chapter 9:
Eyewitness Testimonies
The Nature of Eyewitness Accounts

Eyewitness accounts play a crucial role in shaping public understanding of significant events, particularly traumatic ones like the attacks on September 11, 2001. While these accounts are often viewed as powerful pieces of evidence, their nature is complex and can be influenced by a variety of psychological and situational factors. Understanding the dynamics of eyewitness testimony is essential for analyzing the myriad conspiracy theories surrounding 9/11, as these narratives often rely heavily on personal experiences that may contradict of cial reports.

One of the primary challenges associated with eyewitness accounts is the inherent fallibility of human memory. Psychological research indicates that memories, especially those formed during high-stress situations, can be distorted over time. Factors such as the emotional intensity of the event, the chaotic environment, and subsequent discussions with others can alter an eyewitness's recollection. This phenomenon raises questions about the reliability of the testimonies that emerged in the wake of 9/11, as many individuals reported seeing or experiencing events that directly contradicted the of cial narrative provided by government and media sources.

Furthermore, the context in which these eyewitness accounts are presented can significantly influence their reception. In the aftermath of 9/11, the media played a pivotal role in framing the narratives surrounding the attacks. Eyewitness testimonies were frequently broadcast, often without critical analysis of their context or reliability. This unaltered presentation contributed to the formation of a collective memory that may not accurately reflect the events as they unfolded. For those who later questioned the official accounts, these testimonies became a focal point for alternative narratives, suggesting that the government had either misrepresented or concealed the truth surrounding the attacks.

The implications of eyewitness accounts extend beyond mere factual discrepancies; they also touch on broader societal themes, such as fear and distrust in authority. In a post-9/11 world marked by heightened security measures and ongoing geopolitical tensions, many individuals began to view eyewitness testimonies as evidence of deeper conspiracies. The perception that the government may have been involved in or complicit with the attacks fueled a growing skepticism, leading to a proliferation of conspiracy theories. This distrust was further exacerbated by the media's portrayal of certain eyewitness accounts as sensational or exaggerated, reinforcing the belief that the truth was being manipulated.

Ultimately, analyzing the nature of eyewitness accounts in the context of 9/11 reveals a complex interplay between memory, perception, and societal response. While these testimonies can provide valuable insights into the human experience of trauma, their reliability is often compromised by psychological factors and external influences. As the public continues to grapple with the implications of 9/11, it is essential to critically evaluate the narratives constructed from these accounts, recognizing their role in shaping both individual beliefs and broader societal fears. Understanding the limitations of eyewitness testimony is crucial for unpacking the intricate web of conspiracy theories that have emerged in the years since the attacks, highlighting the ongoing struggle for truth in the face of manipulation and control.

Contradictions with Official Narratives

Contradictions with official narratives surrounding the events of September 11, 2001, have become a focal point for conspiracy theories, sparking debates that question the integrity of governmental accounts and media reports. Many individuals have found themselves drawn to alternative explanations that challenge the official story, suggesting not only a lack of transparency but also a potential cover-up involving key governmental agencies. This subchapter delves into the inconsistencies found within official narratives, illuminating how they have fueled widespread skepticism and distrust among the public.

Eyewitness testimonies play a critical role in shaping perceptions of the 9/11 attacks. Numerous accounts from individuals present during the events contradict official reports regarding the sequence of events, the sounds heard, and even the characteristics of the buildings' destruction. For instance, some witnesses described hearing explosions that seemed to precede the collapse of the Twin Towers, leading to speculation about controlled demolition rather than structural failure due to impact and re. This divergence from the official narrative raises questions about the integrity of the information disseminated by authorities and highlights the potential for manipulation in the aftermath of the attacks.

The media's portrayal of the events surrounding 9/11 further complicates the official narrative. Mainstream outlets rapidly adopted the government's initial explanations, often framing the attacks as a clear-cut case of terrorism orchestrated by al-Qaeda. However, the subsequent lack of critical analysis of these claims has led to accusations of complicity in a broader agenda. By failing to adequately investigate the myriad of inconsistencies, the media played a significant role in shaping public perception, often prioritizing sensationalism over thorough journalism. This relationship between the media and government narratives raises important questions about accountability and the role of the press in a democratic society.

Financial motives also feature prominently in discussions about the contradictions with official narratives. The aftermath of 9/11 saw a surge in military contracts and insurance claims, leading some to speculate whether elements within the government or private sector had something to gain from the attacks. The economic implications of the events have prompted inquiry into whether certain parties had foreknowledge of the attacks, thus allowing them to pro t from the chaos. This intertwining of economic interests with national security raises ethical concerns and invites scrutiny of the motivations behind the governmental response to the attacks.

The role of the military in the events surrounding 9/11 has also been met with skepticism. Claims of foreknowledge or complicity by military officials have surfaced in various conspiracy theories, suggesting that a coordinated effort existed to either allow the attacks to occur or to manage the response in a way that would further specific agendas. As this subchapter explores, these contradictions within the official narrative reveal a complex interplay of fear, manipulation, and control, demonstrating how 9/11 has not only shaped national policy but also transformed the public's perception of truth in an age of information warfare.

Implications for Truth and Credibility

The events of September 11, 2001, have not only shaped global politics but have also given rise to a plethora of conspiracy theories that challenge the official narratives surrounding the attacks. The implications for truth and credibility in this context are profound, as they highlight the complex interplay between perception, belief, and the manipulation of information. Conspiracy theories often emerge in the wake of significant events, particularly when those events evoke strong emotional responses, such as fear and anger. In the case of 9/11, the trauma experienced by the American public created fertile ground for alternative explanations that resonate with deeper societal anxieties about government transparency, security, and the nature of truth itself.

The role of government agencies in the events of 9/11 has been a focal point for many conspiracy theorists who argue that there were failures, cover-ups, or even complicity involved. This skepticism towards official accounts raises critical questions about the credibility of institutions tasked with safeguarding public safety. When government narratives are perceived as inconsistent or incomplete, the trust placed in these institutions erodes, paving the way for alternative explanations that often lack robust evidence. The implications here extend beyond mere speculation; they reflect a growing disillusionment with authority and a demand for accountability that may not always be met, thus perpetuating a cycle of mistrust.

Media manipulation plays a significant role in shaping public perception of events like 9/11. The mainstream media's coverage influenced how the attacks were understood and interpreted, often framing them in a manner that aligned with governmental narratives. However, this alignment has led to accusations of bias and censorship, particularly concerning alternative viewpoints and dissenting voices. The implications for truth arise when the media's portrayal is perceived as a tool for maintaining control rather than providing an accurate account of events. This perceived manipulation fosters a belief that the truth is malleable, leading individuals to seek out information that aligns with their pre-existing beliefs, further polarizing discourse.

Theories surrounding controlled demolition of the Twin Towers and WTC 7 illustrate another layer of complexity in discussions about truth and credibility. Proponents of these theories argue that the physical evidence suggests the use of explosives rather than the impact of planes. Such claims challenge not only the official narrative but also the foundational understanding of structural engineering and safety protocols. The implications for credibility here are significant, as they force a reevaluation of accepted knowledge and highlight the difficulty in discerning fact from fiction in a post-truth world. The debate over controlled demolition exemplifies how scientific discourse can become entwined with ideological beliefs, complicating public understanding.

Finally, the financial motives tied to 9/11, including military contracts and insurance claims, further complicate the conversation about truth and credibility. The argument that certain entities may have financially benefited from the tragedy raises ethical questions about the intersection of profit and disaster response. This perspective feeds into broader conspiracy theories, suggesting that financial gain could have motivated actions or inactions leading up to the attacks. As society grapples with these implications, it becomes clear that the pursuit of truth in the aftermath of 9/11 is not simply about uncovering facts; it is also about understanding the underlying societal fears and distrust that shape collective narratives and beliefs. These layers of complexity illustrate the ongoing struggle for credibility in a world where truth seems increasingly elusive.

Chapter 10:
Foreign Involvement Theories
Investigating Claims of Foreign Government Involvement

The investigation into claims of foreign government involvement in the events of September 11, 2001, necessitates a careful examination of the geopolitical landscape preceding the attacks. Various conspiracy theories suggest that foreign governments or organizations may have orchestrated or facilitated the attacks as part of a larger strategy. Supporters of these theories often cite historical tensions, such as U.S. foreign policy in the Middle East, as a backdrop for potential collusion or manipulation by external actors. The context of these relationships is crucial; they reveal how historical animosities and alliances may provide plausible motivations for certain foreign entities to engage in acts of terrorism or to exploit existing vulnerabilities within the U.S. system.

Central to the discourse on foreign involvement is the role of intelligence agencies and their capacity for foreknowledge. Critics argue that if there were indeed indications of an impending attack, then foreign governments might have had a vested interest in either facilitating or allowing the attacks to occur to achieve their own geopolitical goals. This raises significant questions about the efficacy of U.S. intelligence and whether critical information was overlooked or ignored. The convoluted nature of international relations complicates the narrative, as allegations of foreign complicity often rely on a web of circumstantial evidence rather than definitive proof, leaving room for skepticism and further investigation.

In exploring these theories, it is essential to analyze the testimonies and statements from various insiders, including former intelligence officials and whistleblowers who have claimed knowledge of foreign government involvement or complicity. These accounts, while often dismissed by mainstream narratives, can provide alternative perspectives that challenge the official story. Eyewitness testimonies that contradict established timelines or facts can lend credence to conspiracy theories, as they highlight the potential for manipulation of information by both foreign and domestic actors. However, the reliability of these testimonies is frequently debated, as emotional and psychological factors may color perceptions of the events surrounding 9/11.

The role of the media in shaping public perception of foreign involvement cannot be overstated. Mainstream narratives often focus on blaming specific groups, while neglecting to explore the broader implications of foreign government actions leading up to the attacks. The portrayal of certain nations or ideologies as inherently dangerous can perpetuate fear and influence domestic policy decisions, effectively serving as a form of psychological warfare. This media manipulation not only affects public opinion but also contributes to a climate of distrust in government, where citizens may turn to alternative explanations for the events of 9/11, including those that implicate foreign actors.

Finally, the economic ramifications of 9/11 also feed into theories of foreign involvement. The aftermath of the attacks saw a surge in military spending and defense contracts, creating potential financial incentives for various parties. Questions surrounding the motivations of foreign governments or organizations often intersect with these financial interests, suggesting that economic gain could be a driving force behind orchestrating such catastrophic events. In this context, conspiracy theories surrounding foreign involvement evolve into reflections of broader societal fears and distrust, illustrating how deeply intertwined the narratives of power, manipulation, and control are in the wake of one of history's most significant tragedies.

The Role of Terrorist Organizations

The role of terrorist organizations in the context of 9/11 extends beyond the immediate act of violence; it encompasses a broader narrative of manipulation and control that has lasting implications. These organizations, often motivated by extremist ideologies, seek to instill fear and chaos, leveraging psychological tactics to influence public perception and policy. By examining the actions and motivations of groups like al-Qaeda, one can better understand how their activities have not only shaped the events of that fateful day but also contributed to a myriad of conspiracy theories that have emerged in its aftermath.

Terrorist organizations aim to create a sense of vulnerability within a population, and the attacks on September 11, 2001, exemplified this strategy. The dramatic nature of the assaults—targeting symbols of American power and financial might— was designed to provoke a strong emotional response. This fear has been a critical factor in how various narratives have developed, leading many to question the official accounts of the event. The rise of conspiracy theories regarding 9/11 reflects a societal reaction to the fear instilled by these organizations, as individuals attempt to regain a sense of control and understanding in the face of trauma.

Moreover, the alleged involvement of government agencies in the events of 9/11 has lent credence to various conspiracy theories. These theories often suggest that elements within the U.S. government either had prior knowledge of the attacks or were complicit in them as a means to further specific agendas. This perspective underscores a profound distrust in authority figures, which has been exacerbated by the psychological impact of the attacks. As such, the role of terrorist organizations transcends their immediate actions; they become part of a larger narrative that implicates various societal structures in a web of manipulation and control.

Media manipulation has also played a significant role in shaping public perception of terrorist organizations and the events of 9/11. The mainstream media's portrayal of the attacks, often sensationalized and laden with fear-inducing rhetoric, reinforced the narratives that terrorist organizations aimed to create. This coverage has influenced how the public understands not only the events of 9/11 but also the motivations behind terrorism in general. As viewers consumed these narratives, they became susceptible to a range of beliefs, including those that suggest controlled demolitions and other alternative explanations for the collapse of the World Trade Center buildings.

In conclusion, the role of terrorist organizations in the context of 9/11 is multifaceted, serving as both a catalyst for fear and a focal point for conspiracy theories. The psychological operations that emerged in response to these organizations' actions reflect a deeper societal struggle with distrust, fear, and the quest for truth. By understanding the intricate relationship between terrorist organizations and the narratives that surround 9/11, we can better appreciate the complexities of psychological warfare and its implications for society at large.

Evaluating the Evidence for Foreign Complicity

Evaluating the evidence for foreign complicity in the events surrounding 9/11 requires a careful analysis of various claims and theories that have emerged since that fateful day. Conspiracy theories regarding foreign involvement often suggest that governments or organizations outside the United States played a direct role in orchestrating or facilitating the attacks. These theories frequently cite a range of motivations, from geopolitical strategies to financial gains. While some may dismiss these theories outright, a deeper examination reveals a complex interplay of historical context, political interests, and the psychological impact of fear that shapes public perception.

One of the primary arguments for foreign complicity centers around the alleged involvement of specific countries or intelligence agencies. Some theorists point to the long-standing tensions in the Middle East and the relationships the U.S. maintained with various governments, suggesting that these dynamics created fertile ground for manipulation. Furthermore, the narrative often includes claims of foreknowledge or complicity from foreign intelligence services, which raises questions about the extent to which these organizations might have either actively participated in the attacks or failed to provide critical information that could have prevented them.

The role of the media in shaping the narrative of foreign complicity cannot be understated. In the immediate aftermath of 9/11, mainstream media outlets were quick to report on the alleged connections between the attackers and foreign entities, leading to widespread public belief in these theories. This reporting often relied on sensationalism rather than substantiated evidence, contributing to a climate of fear and suspicion. The portrayal of certain countries as hostile and complicit reinforced existing stereotypes and biases, further entrenching the idea that foreign actors were responsible for the tragedy. This manipulation of information has significant implications for how the public perceives both the events of 9/11 and the broader geopolitical landscape.

Claims of controlled demolition, particularly concerning the Twin Towers and World Trade Center 7, often intersect with theories of foreign involvement. Proponents of this theory argue that the precision of the buildings' collapse could not be attributed solely to the impact of the planes, suggesting instead that explosives were used. This argument is sometimes coupled with assertions that foreign actors could have had the means and motive to facilitate such an operation. While these claims lack definitive evidence, they highlight a broader societal concern regarding trust in governmental narratives and the potential for covert operations that could serve foreign interests.

Finally, the psychological impact of 9/11 conspiracy theories, including those focusing on foreign complicity, reflects a deep-seated distrust in government institutions. The events of that day left many Americans grappling with feelings of vulnerability and fear, creating an environment ripe for conspiracy theories to flourish. As individuals sought to make sense of an incomprehensible tragedy, the notion that foreign powers were involved served as both an explanation and a means of externalizing blame. This dynamic illustrates how fear can drive people to embrace alternative narratives, often regardless of the evidence, as a way to regain a sense of control over their understanding of the world. In this context, evaluating the evidence for foreign complicity requires not only a critical look at the facts but also an understanding of the psychological and societal forces at play.

Chapter 11:
Psychological Operations Denying Psychological Operations (Psyops)

Denying Psychological Operations (Psyops) requires an understanding of their fundamental purpose and methodology within the context of warfare and manipulation. At its core, psyops are strategic communications aimed at influencing the perceptions, emotions, and behaviors of individuals or groups. These operations utilize a variety of media, narratives, and psychological tactics to foster desired responses, often in the context of national security or military objectives. In the aftermath of 9/11, the concept of psyops gained prominence as various narratives emerged regarding the nature of the attacks and the subsequent response by the U.S. government and military.

The role of psychological operations in shaping public perception can be particularly evident in the way the events of 9/11 were framed by both government authorities and mainstream media. Following the attacks, a cohesive narrative was rapidly constructed to unify the American public against perceived threats, which involved the portrayal of terrorism as a dire and imminent danger. This narrative not only justified military action abroad but also facilitated the implementation of domestic policies that expanded governmental powers. By controlling the ow of information and framing the narrative, those in power effectively utilized psyops to consolidate authority and suppress dissent.

Various conspiracy theories surrounding 9/11 exemplify the complexity of psychological operations and their potential impact on public consciousness. Claims regarding government cover-ups, controlled demolitions, and foreign involvement reflect broader societal fears and distrust in institutions. These theories often serve as a counter-narrative to the official explanations, suggesting that the truth is more complex than what is presented by authorities. The persistence of these theories can be attributed to an inherent skepticism among the populace, fueled by historical precedents of governmental deceit and manipulation. They illustrate how psyops can create an environment ripe for speculation and mistrust, complicating the search for truth.

Eyewitness testimonies and alternative accounts further complicate the narrative surrounding 9/11. Many individuals reported experiences that contradicted the official story, adding to the confusion and uncertainty surrounding the attacks. In the context of psyops, such testimonies can be seen as a double-edged sword; they may undermine the established narrative or, conversely, can be weaponized by those manipulating public perception. The credibility and implications of these accounts highlight the challenges faced by both proponents and skeptics of the official story, illustrating the psychological battleground that emerged in the wake of the attacks.

Ultimately, the analysis of 9/11 as a potential psychological operation reveals the intricate interplay between fear, manipulation, and control in the wake of a national crisis. The events of that day not only reshaped the geopolitical landscape but also altered the psychological landscape of the American public. By understanding the mechanisms of psyops, one gains insight into how narratives are constructed, disseminated, and contested in the public sphere. This understanding is crucial for critically evaluating the myriad of theories and claims that have emerged since 9/11, enabling a more nuanced dialogue about the impacts of psychological warfare on society.

9/11 as a Potential Psyop

The events of September 11, 2001, stand as a watershed moment in modern history, marked not only by the tragic loss of thousands of lives but also by a plethora of conspiracy theories that have emerged in its wake. Some theorists argue that the attacks may have been a psychological operation (psyop) designed to manipulate public perception and behavior. This perspective posits that the orchestrators of 9/11 aimed to instill fear and confusion, thereby justifying increased government control and military intervention both domestically and abroad. By examining the broader implications of such a theory, we can better understand how psychological warfare operates in the context of catastrophic events.

In the realm of psychological operations, the role of government agencies becomes a focal point of investigation. Allegations of foreknowledge or even complicity in the events of 9/11 have sparked intense debate. Critics argue that certain government entities may have benefited from the chaos that ensued, using it as a pretext to advance agendas such as the War on Terror. These claims raise profound questions about the extent to which government actions can be viewed as manipulative. If a psyop did occur, it would suggest a calculated effort to exploit public trauma for political gain, raising ethical considerations about the nature of truth in governance.

Media manipulation played a crucial role in shaping the narrative around 9/11. Mainstream media outlets, under immense pressure to report rapidly on the unfolding crisis, often relied on government sources for information. This reliance has been criticized for creating a one-dimensional portrayal of events that sidelined alternative explanations and dissenting voices. The framing of 9/11 in the media not only influenced public perception but also set the stage for the ensuing wars in Afghanistan and Iraq. By analyzing how information was disseminated and controlled, we can better appreciate the potential for psychological manipulation inherent in such a significant event.

Theories surrounding controlled demolition provide another avenue for exploring the psyop narrative. Proponents assert that the collapse of the Twin Towers and World Trade Center 7 could not have occurred solely due to the impact of the planes and subsequent res. They argue that the precision of the collapses and the presence of certain physical evidence indicate a premeditated act involving explosives. This theory highlights the intersection of fear and distrust, as many individuals struggle to reconcile the official account with their own observations and experiences. The insistence on alternative explanations reflects a broader societal skepticism towards authority, particularly in the wake of traumatic events.

Lastly, the financial motives tied to 9/11 warrant attention in the context of psychological warfare. The aftermath of the attacks saw a surge in military contracts, security enhancements, and insurance claims that raised eyebrows regarding who truly bene ted from the tragedy. These economic factors intertwine with conspiracy theories, suggesting that the attacks were not just acts of terrorism but also catalysts for financial gain. This multifaceted approach underscores how 9/11 has become a symbol of manipulation, wherein fear and economic interests converge, prompting a critical examination of the event's legacy in terms of public trust and psychological control.

The Effects of Psychological Manipulation on Society

Psychological manipulation, particularly in the context of significant historical events like 9/11, has profound effects on society that resonate far beyond the immediate aftermath. The events of September 11, 2001, not only resulted in a tragic loss of life but also served as a pivotal moment for psychological warfare, especially through the dissemination of information and narratives that shaped public perception. The manipulation of emotions, such as fear and anger, has been weaponized to influence societal beliefs and behaviors, leading to a landscape ripe for conspiracy theories and a general distrust in government institutions. These psychological tactics have not only affected individual sentiments but have also altered the collective consciousness of society.

One of the most discernible effects of psychological manipulation in the wake of 9/11 has been the rise of conspiracy theories that suggest alternative narratives to the official account of events. Theories regarding government cover-ups abound, with some positing that U.S. agencies had prior knowledge of the attacks or were even complicit in their orchestration. This distrust is fueled by a perceived lack of transparency from the government, leading citizens to question the veracity of of cial reports. As these theories gain traction, they create a societal divide, where individuals align themselves with groups that either endorse or refute these narratives, further entrenching their beliefs.

Media manipulation plays a crucial role in shaping the narratives surrounding 9/11. The mainstream media's portrayal of the events and their aftermath has been scrutinized for its potential biases and the framing of information. The initial coverage was marked by sensationalism and emotional appeals, which served to heighten public fear and urgency. As the media continued to report on the evolving situation, the narratives that emerged often aligned with governmental perspectives, thereby reinforcing the idea that the media is an extension of state power. This convergence of media and government narratives erodes trust and fuels skepticism, prompting individuals to seek alternative sources of information and, consequently, conspiracy theories.

The implications of psychological manipulation extend to the examination of eyewitness testimonies and their credibility. Many individuals reported experiences that contradict the official narrative, leading to a cacophony of conflicting accounts. The prominence of these testimonials in conspiracy discussions highlights how psychological manipulation can influence perception and memory. People may unconsciously align their memories with prevailing narratives or feel pressured to conform to societal expectations, thus complicating the quest for truth. This phenomenon underscores the need for critical thinking and skepticism in assessing information, especially when emotions run high.

Lastly, the impact of fear as a manipulation tool cannot be overstated. After 9/11, fear was not only a natural response but also a strategic tool employed by government and media alike to galvanize public support for military actions and security measures. This pervasive atmosphere of fear has lasting effects on societal trust and cohesion, leading to a climate where dissenting opinions are often marginalized. Financial motives further complicate this dynamic, as the military-industrial complex bene ts from the ongoing state of alert and the resultant government spending. The interplay of fear, economic interests, and psychological manipulation has created a society that is increasingly wary of its own institutions, fostering an environment where conspiracy theories flourish and critical dialogue is stymied.

Chapter 12:
Historical Context
Events Leading Up to 9/11

The events leading up to September 11, 2001, are shrouded in complexity and intrigue, setting the stage for a series of catastrophic occurrences that have since been scrutinized through various lenses, including conspiracy theories and allegations of government complicity. In the years preceding the attacks, a climate of fear and uncertainty had already begun to permeate American society, fueled by various geopolitical tensions and extremist threats. The rise of militant groups, particularly in the Middle East, along with the United States' involvement in regional conflicts, created a backdrop that many conspiracy theorists argue laid the groundwork for the tragic events of 9/11. This atmosphere of crisis and vulnerability would later be leveraged by various entities for manipulation and control.

In the months leading up to 9/11, there were several significant warnings and indicators that have since been interpreted through multiple narratives. Various intelligence agencies reportedly received information about a potential attack, yet the responses were perceived as inadequate. The existence of these warnings, coupled with the subsequent failures to act upon them, has led to speculation about the level of foreknowledge possessed by government officials. Critics argue that such negligence may not have been accidental but rather a calculated move to facilitate a larger agenda. This ambiguity fosters distrust and has contributed to the proliferation of conspiracy theories surrounding the events of that fateful day.

Media coverage of the lead-up to 9/11 also played a crucial role in shaping public perception. The mainstream media's portrayal of terrorism as an imminent threat intensified public anxiety and heightened the sense of vulnerability among Americans. The narratives constructed during this period often omitted critical discussions about U.S. foreign policy and its implications, leading to a simplified understanding of the motivations behind the attacks. As the media quickly pivoted to cover the aftermath of the attacks, significant questions regarding the motivations, potential foreknowledge, and the broader geopolitical context were often overshadowed by sensationalism and fear-driven reporting. This manipulation of information contributed to a societal atmosphere ripe for the acceptance of alternative explanations.

The controlled demolition theories surrounding the Twin Towers and World Trade Center 7 have gained traction in certain circles, with some proponents arguing that the structural failures could not have occurred solely due to the impact of the planes. These theories suggest that explosives were employed to bring down the buildings, implicating a more extensive conspiracy involving government or private entities. The lack of definitive answers regarding the collapse, combined with the dramatic nature of the events, has led many to question the official narrative and seek alternative explanations that align with their pre-existing fears and distrust.

Finally, the financial implications of 9/11 cannot be overlooked, as various industries, particularly defense and security, experienced significant gains in the aftermath of the attacks. Insurance claims, contracts for military operations, and homeland security measures created a lucrative environment for certain sectors, raising questions about the potential motivations behind the events. This intersection of fear, pro t, and manipulation has been a focal point for conspiracy theorists who argue that the attacks served as a catalyst for a broader agenda of control and surveillance. As investigations continue and new evidence emerges, the historical context of the events leading up to 9/11 remains a critical area of examination, revealing the psychological operations at play and the profound impact on American society.

Historical Precedents for Conspiracy Theories

Historical precedents for conspiracy theories reveal a persistent pattern in human behavior, particularly in times of crisis. Throughout history, significant events have often been accompanied by skepticism towards official narratives, leading to the emergence of alternative explanations. This phenomenon can be traced back to critical moments such as the assassination of President John F. Kennedy, the Watergate scandal, and the Gulf of Tonkin incident. Each of these events sparked widespread speculation and conspiracy theories, highlighting a fundamental distrust in governmental institutions and the media. The aftermath of 9/11 has followed this historical trajectory, with a multitude of conspiracy theories surfacing that challenge the accepted accounts of the attacks.

Government cover-ups have played a central role in the proliferation of conspiracy theories. Allegations of involvement by government agencies during 9/11 have fueled speculation about foreknowledge or complicity. The controversial actions of intelligence agencies, such as the CIA and FBI, before and after the attacks have led some to argue that these organizations either failed to act on crucial intelligence or were involved in orchestrating the events. The lack of transparency surrounding investigations and the release of classified documents has further exacerbated public mistrust, allowing conspiracy theories to flourish in the absence of clear answers.

Media manipulation has also significantly shaped the narratives surrounding 9/11. The portrayal of the attacks and their aftermath in mainstream media often reflected a certain bias, emphasizing national security and fear while downplaying dissenting voices. This selective reporting has created a fertile ground for conspiracy theories, as individuals seeking alternative explanations are often met with resistance from traditional media outlets. The tendency to frame the narrative in a way that supports government actions, such as the wars in Iraq and Afghanistan, can lead the public to question the motivations behind the coverage and the integrity of the information being presented.

Controlled demolition theories, which suggest that the Twin Towers and WTC 7 were brought down by explosives rather than the impact of planes, exemplify the intricate relationship between historical precedents and contemporary conspiracy narratives. These theories draw parallels to previous incidents where demolitions were carried out in controlled environments, prompting individuals to scrutinize the evidence and seek alternative explanations for the structural failures observed on 9/11. Eyewitness testimonies that contradict official accounts also lend weight to these theories, as personal narratives challenge the singularity of the mainstream perspective and contribute to a more complex understanding of the events.

Finally, the psychological dimension of conspiracy theories cannot be overlooked. Historical context plays a crucial role in shaping societal fears and distrust, particularly in the wake of traumatic events like 9/11. The lingering impact of fear on public perception is evident in the way individuals interpret information and seek out alternative narratives. Conspiracy theories often reflect deeper anxieties about government control, personal safety, and the unpredictability of global politics. By examining these historical precedents, it becomes clear that conspiracy theories are not merely modern phenomena but rather a continuation of a long-standing human tendency to question authority, especially in the face of crisis and uncertainty.

The Influence of History on Public Perception

The influence of history on public perception is a crucial element in understanding the narratives surrounding the events of September 11, 2001. Historical events shape collective memory and contribute to the frameworks through which people interpret current occurrences. In the context of 9/11, the decades leading up to the attacks are marked by pivotal incidents, such as the Gulf War, the rise of global terrorism, and the U.S. government's involvement in foreign conficts. These historical precedents not only inform public sentiments but also foster an environment ripe for conspiracy theories, as individuals seek to connect past grievances with present realities.

The emotional aftermath of 9/11 played a significant role in shaping perceptions of government credibility and media reporting. In the wake of the attacks, many citizens experienced profound fear and uncertainty, leading to a willingness to accept alternative narratives that provided explanations for the chaos. Notably, the rise of conspiracy theories post-9/11 can be attributed to a widespread distrust in official narratives provided by government agencies and mainstream media, both of which were perceived as potentially complicit in a cover-up. This skepticism is heightened when historical instances of misinformation and manipulation by governments are recalled, reinforcing the belief that powerful entities might have hidden agendas.

Media coverage of the events surrounding 9/11 also illustrates the interplay between history and public perception. The framing of the attacks and the ensuing War on Terror was heavily influenced by the media's portrayal of past threats and conflicts. The rapid dissemination of information, often mixed with sensationalism, shaped public understanding and acceptance of the government's narrative. This pattern is not new; historical instances of media manipulation have been documented throughout wartime, leading to a critical examination of how narratives are constructed and the implications they hold for societal beliefs.

Claims regarding controlled demolitions and the military's role further complicate the historical context of 9/11. Theories suggesting that the Twin Towers and WTC 7 were brought down by explosives rather than aircraft reflect a demand for accountability and a search for alternative explanations that align with existing historical grievances. Concurrently, investigations into the military's actions before and during the attacks have raised questions about foreknowledge or complicity, echoing concerns that have persisted throughout history regarding military transparency and governmental oversight.

The intersection of historical context, psychological operations, and financial motives adds depth to the analysis of public perception regarding 9/11. The economic ramifications of the attacks, including insurance claims and military contracts, invite scrutiny from those who believe that financial interests may have influenced the unfolding of events. Overall, the historical lens through which people view 9/11 continues to shape societal fears and suspicions, creating a complex web of beliefs that persist in the collective consciousness. This interplay between history and perception not only informs current discussions about 9/11 but also underscores the importance of critically examining the narratives that emerge in the aftermath of traumatic events.

Chapter 13:
Conclusion Summary of Key Findings

The subchapter "Summary of Key Findings" encapsulates the multifaceted analysis of the events surrounding September 11, 2001, and its aftermath, revealing a complex interplay of psychological warfare, manipulation, and societal response. This examination highlights the emergence of conspiracy theories as a reflection of public skepticism towards government narratives, fueled by perceived inconsistencies and a lack of transparency. Key findings indicate that these theories, while often dismissed as irrational, tap into deep-rooted fears and mistrust of authority, suggesting that they may resonate with underlying societal anxieties.

One of the central themes in the analysis is the alleged involvement of government agencies in the orchestration or facilitation of the attacks. This includes a dissection of various conspiracy theories that propose active participation or willful negligence on the part of the government. The findings suggest that the convoluted nature of the events, combined with questionable actions taken by agencies prior to and during the attacks, has led to a fertile ground for speculation and distrust. This distrust is further amplified by instances of censorship and the perceived manipulation of information by those in power, leading to a belief that the official narrative may not tell the whole story.

The role of mainstream media in shaping public perception of 9/11 is another critical finding. The initial reporting, characterized by sensationalism and a lack of critical inquiry, played a significant part in establishing the dominant narrative. Subsequent analysis shows that media outlets often prioritized dramatic imagery and emotional responses over factual reporting, leading to a collective psychological imprint that influenced public sentiment. This media manipulation not only shaped the immediate response to the attacks but also laid the groundwork for ongoing narratives that have persisted in the years since.

Moreover, the exploration of controlled demolition theories provides insight into the psychological mechanisms at play. The assertion that the Twin Towers and WTC 7 were brought down by explosives rather than the impact of airplanes reflects a broader anxiety about safety and security in an unpredictable world. The findings indicate that these theories are not merely about the events of that day but are tied to a larger discourse on trust in engineering, government oversight, and the integrity of public institutions. Eyewitness testimonies, often cited as contradictory to official accounts, further complicate the narrative, revealing the subjective nature of perception and memory in high-stress situations.

Finally, the analysis underscores the financial motives intertwined with the aftermath of 9/11, highlighting the economic implications that arose from the tragedy. The examination of military contracts, insurance claims, and the rise of the surveillance state reveals how economic interests can shape policy and public perception. The findings suggest that the interplay of fear, economic gain, and political maneuvering has created a complex landscape in which conspiracy theories thrive, reflecting a society grappling with its understanding of truth and authority. Overall, this subchapter summarizes the critical findings that illuminate the psychological warfare aspects of 9/11, revealing the intricate layers of human response to trauma, manipulation, and control.

The Ongoing Impact of 9/11 Conspiracy Theories

The events of September 11, 2001, not only reshaped global politics and security measures but also gave rise to an array of conspiracy theories that continue to influence public perception and discourse. The ongoing impact of these theories reflects a complex interplay of societal fears, distrust in government institutions, and the media's role in shaping narratives. As individuals grapple with the profound consequences of 9/11, conspiracy theories have emerged as a means of making sense of a chaotic world, often leading to a fragmented understanding of reality. This subchapter examines the multifaceted impact of 9/11 conspiracy theories on society, highlighting their psychological, sociopolitical, and cultural implications.

One significant aspect of 9/11 conspiracy theories is the notion of government cover-ups, which posits that various U.S. government agencies played a role in the attacks or failed to act on intelligence that could have prevented them. This perspective thrives in an environment of skepticism toward official narratives, fueled by historical instances of government malfeasance. The belief that shadowy figures within the government orchestrated the events of that day taps into a deep-seated mistrust among the populace, often exacerbated by perceived inconsistencies in the government's accounts. Such theories not only challenge the credibility of institutions but also encourage citizens to question the motives behind governmental actions, further deepening societal divisions.

Media manipulation plays a crucial role in the propagation of 9/11 conspiracy theories. The mainstream media's portrayal of the events and subsequent narratives has often been criticized for lacking critical analysis and for reinforcing official accounts without sufficient scrutiny. The rapid dissemination of information, coupled with sensationalist reporting, created a fertile ground for misinformation to flourish. In this context, conspiracy theories gained traction, as alternative narratives emerged to ill perceived gaps in the mainstream discourse. This phenomenon highlights the power of media in shaping public perception and underscores the importance of critical media literacy in an age where information is readily accessible yet often misleading.

Controlled demolition theories, which assert that the Twin Towers and World Trade Center 7 were brought down by explosives rather than the impact of airplanes, have gained a significant following among conspiracy theorists. Proponents of this theory often cite the appearance of the buildings' collapse and the scientific principles of engineering to support their claims. This perspective draws on the notion that the official of cial explanation is insufficient and that a deliberate act of destruction was orchestrated to achieve specific political or economic ends. By examining the evidence and arguments presented by both sides, one can better understand the psychological underpinnings of such beliefs and the extent to which they reflect broader anxieties about safety and control in the post-9/11 world.

The military's response to the events of 9/11 has also been a focal point for conspiracy theorists, particularly regarding claims of foreknowledge or complicity. These narratives often suggest that military official had prior knowledge of the attacks and either allowed them to happen or actively participated in them to justify subsequent military interventions. Such theories resonate with individuals who harbor fears about the militarization of society and the potential for government overreach. They reveal a deep-seated concern about the balance of power between the state and its citizens, highlighting how psychological operations may be employed to manipulate public sentiment and justify actions taken in the name of national security.

In conclusion, the ongoing impact of 9/11 conspiracy theories is a testament to the complexities of human psychology and the societal dynamics that shape our understanding of significant events. Whether driven by a desire for truth, a reaction to fear, or a need for control, these theories continue to resonate within various segments of society.

They serve as a reminder of the critical importance of transparency, accountability, and open dialogue in fostering a well-informed citizenry capable of navigating the intricate landscapes of both history and contemporary events. As we reflect on the legacy of 9/11, it is essential to engage with these theories thoughtfully and critically, recognizing their implications for our collective psyche and the future of democratic discourse.

Future Directions for Research and Understanding

Future directions for research and understanding in the context of 9/11 and its implications for psychological warfare are vast and multifaceted. As the landscape of conspiracy theories, government accountability, and media narratives continues to evolve, it is crucial to adopt a comprehensive approach that incorporates various disciplinary perspectives. Future research should not only focus on the events of that fateful day but also on the societal and psychological rami cations that have unfolded in the years since. By examining these interconnected elements, researchers can develop a more nuanced understanding of how psychological manipulation has been employed in both the immediate aftermath and the long-term narrative surrounding 9/11.

One promising avenue for exploration is the intersection of conspiracy theories and psychological operations. Researchers can delve deeper into the mechanisms by which these theories gain traction within public discourse. This includes investigating the psychological needs that drive individuals toward these narratives, such as a desire for certainty in uncertain times or a need to attribute agency to complex events. By understanding the psychological motivations behind belief in conspiracy theories related to 9/11, future studies can inform more effective communication strategies that address public fears and misinformation.

Another important direction is the analysis of media manipulation and its role in shaping public perception. Investigating how mainstream media reported on the events of 9/11 and the subsequent narratives offers insights into the dynamics of trust in information sources. Future research can focus on the methodologies employed by the media and their potential complicity in perpetuating government narratives while sidelining alternative viewpoints. This includes a critical examination of how visual imagery, language, and framing can influence audience reception and understanding of complex events like 9/11, thereby contributing to the broader held belief of media studies and psychological warfare.

The role of eyewitness testimonies is also ripe for further investigation. While some narratives have been challenged, the credibility and implications of these accounts remain significant. Future research should assess not only the reliability of eyewitness testimonies but also the psychological factors that influence memory and perception. Understanding how trauma, stress, and social dynamics affect eyewitness accounts can provide valuable insights into the broader implications of public memory and historical narrative construction.

Finally, exploring the historical context leading up to 9/11 can shed light on the various conspiracy theories that have emerged. By situating the events of September 11, 2001, within a broader historical framework, researchers can identify patterns of governmental action, military involvement, and economic interests that may have contributed to the environment of suspicion and fear. This historical analysis can foster a better understanding of how past events inform contemporary beliefs and fears, ultimately enriching the discourse surrounding 9/11 and its aftermath. The fusion of historical context, psychological analysis, and media studies will provide a holistic approach to understanding the enduring impact of 9/11 on society and the manipulation of public perception.

Don't miss out!

Visit the website below and you can sign up to receive emails whenever Digby R. Kerr publishes a new book. There's no charge and no obligation.

https://books2read.com/r/B-A-BKGHC-ODGYE

BOOKS2READ

Connecting independent readers to independent writers.

Also by Digby R. Kerr

The Ripple Effect

The Ripple Effect: "A Fable About Embracing Change and Thriving in Uncertainty"

The Ripple Effect: "A Fable About Embracing Change and Thriving in Uncertainty"

Standalone

The Universal Code: Unlocking the Secrets of Happiness, Wealth, and Health

Mastering LinkedIn: A Comprehensive Guide to Building Your Profile, Growing Your Audience, and Leveraging Business Opportunities

The Universal Code: Unlocking the Secrets of Happiness, Wealth, and Health

Cross-Border Trade Compliance: Navigating the Global Marketplace

Report on Trends and Challenges in Logistics Hiring

"12 Steps to Success: Real-Life Stories of Manifestation and Transformation"

Psychological Warfare: 9/11 as a Tool for Manipulation and Control

Watch for more at https://www.linkedin.com/in/digbyrkerr/.

About the Author

About the Author

Digby R. Kerr Founder, President & CEO of Logistics Consulting, Inc.Partnered with & Powered by the R+R Group, Family of Companies

Digby R. Kerr is a distinguished global logistics expert and entrepreneur whose profound journey has been marked by both triumphs and trials. From his early life in Borehamwood, London, to his rise in New York and beyond, Digby's path has been a testament to the transformative power of universal principles and personal resilience.

A lifelong learner and seeker of wisdom, Digby has delved deeply into the mysteries of happiness, wealth, and health, drawing from a wealth of knowledge, personal experiences, and interactions with leading experts in psychology, neuroscience, and spirituality. His insights into universal thought and processes have shaped his approach to life and business, guiding him through challenges and leading him to a life of abundance and fulfillment.

In his book, **"Unlocking the Secrets of Happiness, Wealth, and Health,"** Digby shares the transformative teachings and practical strategies that have profoundly impacted his life. By revealing the principles that have helped him navigate his own journey, he offers readers a roadmap to unlock their own potential and achieve their desires. His story is not just one of success but of deep personal transformation, illustrating how understanding and applying universal principles can lead to extraordinary results.

Connect with Digby R. Kerr LinkedIn: Digby R. KerrEmail: DKNYPublishing@icloud.comWebsite: DKNY Publishing

Discover more about Digby's journey, his groundbreaking work, and how his publishing company supports rising star authors with expert guidance and professional support.

Read more at https://www.linkedin.com/in/digbyrkerr/.